TRAITS AND EMOTIONS OF A SALVAGEABLE SOUL

Traits and Emotions of a Salvageable Soul

A Conversation with a Touch of Class

KEESHAWN C. CRAWFORD

PORTLAND • OREGON
inkwaterpress.com

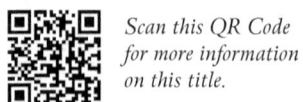

Scan this QR Code
for more information
on this title.

Publisher: Inkwater Press | www.inkwaterpress.com

Paperback ISBN-13 978-1-62901-520-0 | ISBN-10 1-62901-520-2
Hardback ISBN-13 978-1-62901-659-7 | ISBN-10 1-62901-659-4
Kindle ISBN-13 978-1-62901-521-7 | ISBN-10 1-62901-521-0

3 5 7 9 10 8 6 4 2

Dedication

I dedicate this book to my wife, La'Shanda Crawford. For without you the world may never have known the richness of my heart or the depth of my intellect.

God has placed us together for a reason. Some day in the near future, I pray that we may be blessed to learn what that reason is.

Your sacrifices, love, and compassion have taught me to be an example to those who are in need of a guiding hand. I thank you sincerely for showing me how to shine brighter.

Contents

Introduction

I'VE BEEN CONVINCED. Life is entirely too short for any of us to continue thriving solely on personal perceptions, while pretending to ignore the reality of others' existence and significant contributions.

Yes, you've caught me in the act again. In my defense, I just want to help someone other than myself. After writing my first book, *Reclaimed: Everlasting Wisdom*, I felt an overwhelming need to write another book that could serve as inspiration to people who are always searching for that special word. I know I barely allowed the ink from my last book to dry before becoming excited to unleash more food for thought. I hope that's okay. My mind felt obligated to express the emotions of my heart, and so my fingers took off writing.

Please do not take anything that you may not agree with personally. My only intention is to remind the world that we all have a remarkably intrinsic value. The way I see it, although women are the foundation of sensibility, the compassion behind the healing of tormented hearts, and the logic behind man's periodic irrational thinking, it will take all of us together, both young and old, to make the world a better place to live.

Creating this book has provided me with an opportunity to remind the world why we should refrain from questioning the moral teachings of our elders. Before we can expect to evolve, we must learn how to listen to those who know a few things.

Be honest. There's something soothing about an older person's wisdom. It's healing, irregardless of what color your skin may happen to be. Truth? On many occasions I've sat patiently listening and absorbing the logic behind elders' observations. It's my obligation to pass this on to those who may be in need.

This book isn't meant to highlight anyone's shortcomings. I simply want to offer a touch of inspiration to those who are seeking and may be able to benefit from a guiding light while in a dark period of time. At the end of each chapter, you will find a Jewel. These are afterthoughts for you to ponder.

Yes, it is true. None of us knows everything, but we all should be willing to learn how to conduct ourselves in a manner that will make it more pleasurable for others to follow our lead.

I hope that you enjoy the book and don't forget to share with someone who may also have the potential to become a giant.

TRAITS AND EMOTIONS OF
A SALVAGEABLE SOUL

What Enduring Qualities Can Be Found Amongst Beautiful Flowers?

....

Character contributes to beauty. It
fortifies a woman as her youth fades.
A mode of conduct, a standard
of courage, discipline, fortitude
and integrity can do a great deal
to make a woman beautiful.

–JACQUELINE BISSET

....

TO ALL QUEENS of the world, it is truly an
honor to create and dedicate this prominent
exposition solely for your pleasure.

Life adores you. For without you, Mother Nature
might lose her ambition to continually beautify the
planet. Every woman is uniquely special in her own
way. You are a work of exceptional art, a masterpiece
that has always conveyed selflessness, depth, and the
power of healing. Your influence is as magical as your

touch. A touch that communicates the essence of loyalty and concern for all.

So many fail to recognize that you are more precious than all of the world's riches. What potential would any tree have without strong roots to nourish it? We love you. Even in the moments when you cannot muster up the needed strength to love yourself, we have your back. No, we don't always display such emotional tenderness, in part, due to man's mental weakness, which becomes so apparent by way of our inability to articulate our sufferings and frustration when those moments arise. My apologies.

There could never be any justification for others' transgressions or violations against you. How does one contemplate causing pain to the woman who has complemented his life in so many ways? It is hard to fathom. Let me guess, his plea went a little like this: "Sweetheart, I'm sorry. I promise that it will never happen again!" It sounds less than authentic, and so it is I who fearlessly stands atop Mount Everest proclaiming the most sincere apology on behalf of all who have failed to recognize your compassion and generous nature. I beg your forgiveness on behalf of those who have been evil, violent, and intolerable towards your existence, yesterday, today, and tomorrow.

> A fool will never become convinced
> that he should discard his prejudices.
> —LA'SHANDA C. CRAWFORD

The countless contributions to humanity that you

continually make have not fallen upon deaf ears or lost souls. You must conjure up the strength to continue pushing forward, sacrificing, and loving even in the moments when you have convinced yourself you just don't have any more love to give.

There are a few of us left who understand that if we are to embrace your trust, it will mean that we have to be completely comfortable with our emotions in your hands, okay with listening more intently, refrain from creating excuses for our inactions, assisting in building you up and supporting you, as opposed to shattering you and then abandoning you. It means showering you with genuine affection, instead of bombarding you with soul-crushing epithets.

Every woman is worthy of knowing the taste of spellbinding passion and respect on a beautiful level. It's important for you to know how it feels to be the recipient of affection in public, no matter who's secretly admiring you, wishing they had the same. Even when others fail to acknowledge such a truth, you must be strong enough to remind yourself that you are extremely important, regardless of what your current circumstances may be. Hold your head up high and think nothing but positive thoughts about yourself. Walk your walk, and do it with dignity. You're not damaged. I know he tried hard to convince you that you were, but trust me, it was only a high-strung display of stupidity.

You, as so many other precious flowers, are just in need of a healing touch from a true botanist, one who is capable of offering nourishment, replenishment, and restoration that will assist you with regaining your balance. Nothing in existence is without a time for reenergizing. Do not be of the opinion that so convincingly had you believing that you needed a significant other to validate your self-worth. Your happiness, your dignity, your truth, and your self-respect are all inside of you, if only you would search deep enough with the intent to discover what you have always known.

The boys you welcome into your life, due to being afraid of knowing loneliness, they aren't ready yet. See, they have yet to evolve into responsible men. This is part of the reason why you have not been able to function coherently together as one yet. Stop giving passes to boys masquerading as men. If their thoughts, speech, and actions do not conform to those of real men, then they shouldn't in any way be suitable for you.

No real man would ever abuse you physically, mentally, or emotionally. Don't ever tolerate such behavior. A monster will forever be a monster. If he abuses you once, it's only a matter of time before he abuses you again. Think about it. How can a sick person be expected to get well without the help of someone who specializes in infirmities? Never allow people's words to persuade you, but look to their actions for authentication of what they profess.

Your presence is inspirational with a magical pull that's engulfed in a radiant glow. Your soul is resilient. Your personality captivating. Your smile—it is prettier than the stars lining the heavens!

Demand for your mind and body to be respected at all times. Attract what is good for you and quickly turn away from people who are potentially harmful. Should someone find interest in you, let it be due to the recognition of your strong mind and the unrelenting character that has propelled you through troubled waters for so many years. Let him not mistake you for being an opportunity to satisfy his beastly desires. Smile with great confidence when overlooking the snide remarks and the snickering of those who find fault in you for choosing a path of celibacy.

Do not liken yourself to the young woman who was overheard sobbing because her heart continued to ache due to a lost love. Sadly, she had become convinced her life was, from that day forward, forever useless. You will know when Mr. Right comes along. Ethics will elevate his thoughts to a plateau where only true love and a dying loyalty only for you reside. Real affection will obliterate any notion of him not being in sync with you. Then and only then will you know what it is to be soulmates.

Respect yourself, and others will cherish you. Love yourself, for only you know the correct way. There isn't anything that anyone can do for you that would render you incapable of doing for yourself. Do you need to be reminded of the power you behold? Reclaim the wisdom of Queen Makeda of Sheba, Helen A. Keller, Queen Nefertari-aahmes, Maria Montessori, Queen Tetisheri, Florence Nightingale, Queen Nzinga, Harriet Tubman, Mary Dyer, Ida B. Wells, Susan Brownell Anthony, Winnie Madikizela-Mandela, Sojourner Truth, and so many other strong women who have paved the way.

Take care of yourself, and the rest will become much easier.

 **JEWEL**

Strength and honor
are her clothes; and
she shall rejoice in
time to come.

—PROVERBS 31:25

True beauty lies in
the attractiveness
of your soul.

—MS. RE'NEE TAYLOR.

The Way to Happiness

....

The road to happiness lies in two
simple principles: find what it is that
interest you and that you can do well,
and when you find it, put your whole
soul into it- every bit of energy and
ambition and natural ability you have.

– JOHN D. ROCKEFELLER III

....

HAPPINESS—IT IS SELECTIVE when choosing who to minister to. Not everyone has a heart that is worthy of knowing the comforts of such a wonderful pleasure. There are many people who have been afflicted with total darkness, a darkness where grotesque ailments envision the face of their own demonic reality while basking in the perversions and evilness of self-created chaos every single day!

True happiness is a rarity. How could a virtue as indispensable as happiness find eternal bliss in the souls of those who go through life only pretending to honor and respect its essence?

Happiness is not something that can be instilled in you by someone else. It is not something that's capable of being purchased, even if the price entailed the monetary equivalent of all the gold currently deposited inside Fort Knox. Those who erroneously think they are able to discover happiness through the accumulation of materialistic objects prove to be the most discontent of all.

Happiness comes from being comfortable and at peace within yourself. The act of living vicariously through someone else's happiness is nothing more than a mirage, one that could never amount to be anything more than temporary.

We must each conjure up the strength to search for our own silver linings, ones that will cause us to awaken and greet each new day with gracious smiles originating deep down inside. That is a joy no one can ever deprive you of, unless you permit the haters, the nay-sayers, or the energy thieves to strip you of your piece of heaven while here on earth.

A high IQ is not required to understand that through the gateway of positive thoughts, good health, unrestrained love, and acts of selflessness, you may become acquainted with happiness. How else can you explain the euphoric feeling we experience when our emotions become more exciting than a display of fireworks on the Fourth of July?

Without knowledge of how to obtain lasting peace of mind and emotional health to encourage us to smile from the heart, we often find ourselves desperately searching for and indulging in all of the wrongs things, just for the sake of gaining a taste of temporary joy. If only we would slow down enough to recognize the harm we cause ourselves when chasing after ill-gotten wealth and sensuality that only caters to our lower desires. It is in our best interests to understand that through being authentic in every aspect of our lives, we can find true happiness and peace luxuriously entwined in the comforts of our souls. These are a few elementary secrets for the attainment of happiness. It is impossible to enjoy a lasting satisfaction with others if you have yet to discover it for yourself.

"To be of service to others" should be the motto for those of us who pray to someday become acquainted with one of many roads to a lasting happiness. Think for a moment. What could be better than realizing you have given a kid a secure reason to smile and feel safe while in the midst of uncertainties? Children are the most innocent and purest of the world. Why couldn't true happiness be discovered in being the gatekeeper for the world's second most precious jewel (elders being the most precious jewel)? The energy emitted from their personal happiness attracts the best in us all, unless it is your heart that knows all too well the pangs of pettiness.

No one can enjoy the company of those who are grouchy and have a nasty disposition. When a child shows genuine emotion by asking you, "Why are you sad?" In that instant, you cannot help but to smile, and in that smile resides the epitome of genuine happiness. It is a happiness that you will have to search for and find on your own. It may not be discovered today or anytime soon, but it's your journey, and as long as you continue to search for it, you shall find it. Funny thing, sometimes, after it becomes much too late, you make the discovery that it was sitting in front of you all along. You didn't say anything, so what obligation did it owe to you to avail itself? Slow down and follow the direction of the signs.

Try to remember that your cheerful nature can be an inspiration and serve as motivation for others. Do not make life any harder than it has to be. Offer the gift of a smile to those who look as if they are down and out. It may be the lift they are in need of.

Lastly, never forget that happiness is contingent upon who you are as a person. You know, the quality of your heart, as opposed to what you possess materialistically. Happiness is achievable if it's truly what you want.

 **J E W E L**

Happiness lives in the heart. It's a matter of being genuine enough to allow it to arise.

Love Is Unique

LOVE IS MULTIDIMENSIONAL. It can also be profound, yet unbelievably elusive. It's attractive with an extremely comforting feeling to those of us who are unpretentious. It is worthy of appreciation for being a model of how we are supposed to exemplify its qualities without preconditions. Love is possessing the courage to extend trust, in spite of others' shortcomings. It is often a prayer in disguise, waiting for the correct moment to be given life by those who know how to be reciprocal. Periodically, it becomes questionable to those who are already leery of its sincerity. It is lavish by nature; that is, until someone comes along and tampers with the essence of its genuineness. Love is arguably one of the most precious virtues ever bestowed upon us.

Much is to be considered when faced with determining who is, or is not, worthy of our love. Under normal circumstances, family is given an automatic reprieve from consideration, unless a particular member has committed an act of betrayal so grievous it warrants us to forever erase the memory of having once loved or known him/her.

It is a proven fact that those we love the most have the ability to hurt us the worst. So, what are we to do in an attempt to prevent feeling the pain of a broken heart? For starters, learn to love yourself. That's right. Make it a priority to fully embrace who you are, before you contemplate loving someone else. You will never be able to cherish a person the way he/she deserves until you are able to completely love yourself unconditionally.

When you have major love for yourself, you will not permit others to walk over you, talk to you disrespectfully, or dismiss your contributions as being insignificant. Step up and speak your mind. No one who truly loves you would ever say or do anything that would degrade you in any way. No exceptions and certainly no excuses!

In loving ourselves it's important to be discerning. Only through recognizing the qualities and actions of good-hearted people can we trust with great confidence that we are capable of knowing who is worthy of our love. When you are a special individual, it will show, not only in your mannerisms, but in the quality of your relationships.

Never be in a haste to embrace a love that reeks of falseness. What's the hurry? Yes, life is short, but we have the most compassionate God on our side. His love is the most consistent and unconditional, so why so little faith in his timetable for what is to be when it comes to us? Because of our love being an enchanting expression of what we feel, boundaries must be established to prevent others from taking advantage of what we emotionally have to offer. Sometimes, the love that emanates from us attracts unfitting attention. Unfitting in the sense that it comes from people who mean us no good and possess an unmistakable inability to complement our authenticity in any way. Leave them be! You are better off without their false affection. Exchange pleasantries if you must and continue moving along. To you be your way and to them be theirs.

Please watch where you walk. We all should be well aware of the savages lurking in the forest. They will sense your righteousness and smell the pleasant scent of your compassionate loyalty. Curious, they will befriend you while pretending all along to have endured struggles that were similar to yours. In their minds, you are nothing more than vulnerable prey. When the time is appropriate, they will ferociously abuse you, leaving you mentally, physically, and emotionally scarred forever. The depths of your pain will then become the cause of your unwillingness to step foot in a place as beautiful as the forest again.

Today is a perfect day to look in the mirror and forgive yourself for all of your mistakes. The mistakes of yesterday, today, and tomorrow. Try to understand the wrongs you've committed against your being. Make a promise to never travel down such a dangerous path again.

Should you fall in love, don't allow the passion that yearns for expression to distort your rational judgement. Have patience while paying close attention to what your soul finds to be comforting. Know with certainty what has caused you to smile such a beautiful smile without concessions.

Aside from your parents, spouse, or your children, never love anyone more than you love yourself. When a person of interest claims to love you before they know all there is to know about you, they are lying! How could they? A single conversation that truthfully captures all of the unpleasant battles you have been through in life is sure to send them running with no intentions of ever returning.

Many people will immediately pretend to love you only because you have something that is beneficial to them. When whatever it was that initially attracted them to you is gone, watch to see how long it takes before they disappear. Only then will you know for certain that you were never loved for who you are.

When it becomes known that you possess riches beyond that of your mind and soul, evilness will expose its face and people will begin to change without the slightest warning. Should you find yourself strongly attracted to a person who has true potential in character, help to develop that person for the contentedness of your heart and the pleasing of your spirit. You will never have regrets when love is discovered through the depths of your personal happiness. This is what makes love so unique.

 **JEWEL**

Love should never hurt more than it feels good!

–PATRICIA ANN CRAWFORD

There Is No Shame in Helping to Restore Others

As soon as healing takes place, go
out and heal somebody else.

—MAYA ANGELOU

DON'T BE IN such a hurry to think everyone is out to harm you more than you have already been hurt or to detract from what little you have left emotionally. Despite what you may think, there are men and women who will enter your life with the intention of doing nothing more than helping to restore you to a healthy condition. They only want to witness your soul smiling again.

The pain in your eyes is so obvious and your walk is overly protective. It is probably extremely hard to even conceive of someone wanting moments of pleasure to be strictly about you. It is so possible.

Whether it be a day spent shopping or a serene picnic on a quilt at the park, the return of your joy is an acknowledged privilege for the person who has come to restore and an opportunity to experience inner calm for the one who's most in need, you!

Give people a taste of your trust. Just a little bit at a time. Those who truly come to restore will have no gripes with authenticating their intent. Don't be rude and dismissive by pushing away someone special who has just as many beautiful qualities as you. The gift of a restorer is rare. Whether you are restoring an injured soul or you're the beneficiary of such sincere treatment, always be appreciative and show your gratitude. No one wants to live life alone, so it is imperative that you be gentle in your restoration, regardless of whether you are the healer or the recipient of the healing.

Sometimes we go through troubling situations and find ourselves depleted of essential qualities. This prevents us from functioning meaningfully. Without noticing, a healer is needed to help restore our mental, spiritual, and emotional value. No, there isn't an immense variety of people who are caring and self-less enough to qualify to be restorers. This is more of a reason to count your blessings. A true healer only wants to stop the pain and create a space that allows for the restoration of your balance.

....
*Someone's scars are what we
use to cure our disease.*
—AKAN PROVERB
....

No matter how shattered you think you are, there will always be someone who is genuinely concerned enough to remind you that you are in possession of the ability to revitalize yourself. If it's what you really want.

We all have remnants of a fragmented culture deep within, and all that those remnants know is the power of resilience. Our spirits are well connected to the universal force, and this is what helps us bounce back stronger than we were initially. Don't you recognize that we all have souls that echo cries from pains that can sometimes be indescribable? Acknowledge you are in need of intensive healing and speak with passion to what it is that you are feeling. Go ahead, don't hold it back. Explore its depths. When you are honestly ready to be restored, it will be oodles of love that will help you to recognize the pleasure of becoming well again.

 **JEWEL**

You are truly worth restoring.

Sometimes You Will Have To Sacrifice Much

....

A thieving spirit cannot be
appeased by sacrifice.

—NGŨGĨ WA THIONG'O

....

LIFE REQUIRES US to make many sacrifices in an attempt to help enrich the lives of others and to ultimately transcend to a place of serenity.

We sacrifice our time so others who are in need may somehow benefit. We sacrifice our love to remind certain people of how special we consider them to be to us. We sacrifice our compassion so those who are worthy never know what it's like to be abandoned in a time of crisis, and some of us sacrifice our personal comforts in an attempt to prevent others from knowing what it feels like to go without.

True sacrifice is an act of selflessness. We sacrifice, not for the potential of being rewarded, but because deep down inside we know it's the right thing to do. It is what reminds us that we are caring and continue to be full of life.

People make selfish decisions all the time. Some due to pure ignorance, others because they lack concern for the growth and well-being of those they are close to. These are the same people who act as if they know what true friendship is about. They don't have the slightest clue what it means to sacrifice anything, but they'll have the nerve to look down on you with an arrogant attitude, acting as if they are so much greater than you are. Be better to others than others have been to you.

Sacrificing is about having the will to share yourself to better a cause or for the benefit of a person who's in need of stringent guidance, without considering what it might cost you, what you may have missed out on, or where you might be if it weren't for your tender ability to give of yourself so freely.

God has a miraculous way of positioning us at the right place at a time that is most appropriate. The grand scale is so much bigger than we could ever imagine. We must become examples for the betterment of mankind. Thinking, teaching, loving, showing compassion, being generous, and obtaining knowledge that can assist the next man or woman are all free of charge. As a person who understands the beauty of such virtues, how significant would it be if you were to sacrifice your time in order to teach five people what you now know?

It would take dedication, patience, honesty, and a true passion for wanting to see others become better than what they are.

....

You will not be able to do better
if you do not recognize the
importance of becoming better.

−LA'SHANDA C. CRAWFORD

....

For those who now know what it means to be more, do not lose sight of the fact that you too were once without the proper guidance to enable you to know the correct way to go.

You are intelligent. It is important for you to understand that those who once attempted to fight you because you were trying to help them become better were suffering from emotional scars that may not so easily permit the embracing of others without leeriness of their intentions. Even those who couldn't find their way before you have suffered from a psychosis without knowing the seriousness of it.

Think. How is the person who has an unnoticeable drug addiction supposed to seek assistance in getting well if he/she has no consciousness of being sick? When someone who cares about the person directs his/her attention to the fact the person may need help, then and only then will he/she become conscious that something is wrong and consider that it may be time to seek professional help.

Now you should be able to see the importance in sacrificing your wisdom and time as it relates to helping others become mentally stronger. Not for your sake, but for their personal longevity. Be certain to never sacrifice *yourself* for anyone who is unworthy or has no inclination to become a better person for *himself/herself.*

JEWEL

Sacrificing will teach you the essence of humility.

—ANYE CRAWFORD

The Wonders
of Parenting

....

Every parent teaches as they act.

– KEMETIC PROVERB

....

WHAT'S WRONG? WHY the sad face, with tears of despair? I'm certain you have done your absolute best with what you had to work with. Don't be so hard on yourself. People will be quick to say they understand the responsibilities of being a parent, but it's really a ploy that's utilized to secretly critique what you consider to be your finest duty ever.

Parenting is something remarkable. Sure, for most it comes with an abundance of struggles and sacrifices, and with a need for a lot of patience. No parent is perfect. In fact, your shortcomings may often leave you wondering if it was all worthwhile. Of course it was. Be honest; you wouldn't trade the lessons of parenting for anything in the world.

Think of the sleepless nights that have consisted of changing soiled diapers, endless burping sessions, feeding in the wee hours, and cries for a desire to be held close to a caring heart. Wow, what a priceless experience, one that has introduced you to challenging responsibilities, love at its finest level, and a real prospect for what may someday be your greatest achievement yet.

Being a mother or a father to a child is serious business. It is a full-time job that requires you to be on call twenty-four hours a day, seven days a week, for at least eighteen years straight, without compromising. This is what you signed up for, so don't become so easily discouraged when things become a little complicated.

We often fail to realize that it is in the tender moments of conception when it becomes crucial to seriously ponder what shall become of your child. A normal, well-nourished upbringing of a baby requires the guidance of responsible parents who are loving and substantially committed to being involved in their child's life. Not part of the time, but all of the time!

It's important for you to initiate rich discussions about the interests your children have. Discover everything that may provide them with meaningful challenges and joys of contentment. Perhaps they hold ambitions of becoming world-class composers, grandmaster chess players, computer technicians, or scientists. You will never know for certain if you don't make time to probe their wildest fantasies. Even absent a vision that would allow for expression of such greatness, it is incumbent upon all parents to make sure their children are offered the opportunity to participate in some type of after-school activities—piano lessons, the swim team, track and field, karate class, or if nothing else, a persuasive nudge in the direction of the community library will do wonders. Constantly challenge their minds to see what may lie dormant.

Are you aware that influences unfamiliar to many of us await the arrival of every child who is introduced to the world? It's a very subtle influence, one that can be felt urging children to go in the wrong direction. Without the guidance of loving parents, our children can later in life become casualties of their own circumstances. Consider the trance-like state of mind we have all found ourselves in due to listening to rap music or following behind the wrong people, or because we have been consumed with reading material with absolutely no educational value to it. Such garbage captivates and misleads the youth in the opposite direction of where we would love to see them go.

When we don't provide our children with meaningful outlets to help them fully cultivate and develop their talents, it becomes a time of vulnerability, and then environmental influences creep in to mislead them to a dark place.

You may have provided your children with all of the moral teachings in the world, but what happens when your children go off to school on their own? They become easily influenced by the kids they perceive as being "cool." You know, the kids who don't have as much discipline. No home training. No respect for authority. No inclination to listen. These are the kids who sometimes come with a truckload of bad experiences and no one concerned enough to guide them in the right direction. And so they are found lurking around, waiting to indoctrinate the kids who have yet to discover who they are. Heartbreaking, I know. The many sacrifices you have made for the well-being of your children will have been in vain.

Get involved and stay involved in your children's education. Make sure you are vocal. Speak to your children's teachers and be informed. If you don't show concern for their development, why should anyone else feel a need to do so?

Do parent-teacher conferences help? Yes, they usually do. This is an opportunity afforded to you so you will be able to better understand what your children's strengths and weaknesses are. You owe it to them to do what's in your power to continually nurture and stimulate their mental growth. Be the concerned parent who strongly feels a need to challenge their thinking and comprehension skills.

You have been given the guidelines for creating an aspiring professional; now provide the correlation for your children. Show them through your actions how to be strong and assertive yet respectful to all. Be sure to encourage your children's talents. Provide them with an extra dose of love and praise, and a heap of affection. Hug them tight every chance that you get and never fail to remind them of how proud they make you. Let them know how much you love them and how much you trust in them to make the right decisions. Sign it all with a kiss and a delightful smile.

JEWEL

The most important
thing a father can
do for his children is
love their mother.

–THEODORE HESBURGH

Strength Is What Pushes You Through the Rough Times

....

When you are able to demonstrate
that the scent of your existence
is pleasant, you will never be
without honorable rewards.

–QUIMYLL BALLARD

....

WHO ARE YOU that your moral fortitude
shouldn't be searched for traces of weakness or the authenticity of your professed
strength? How will you ever know the deficiency of
your traits if you don't possess strength that's sustainable? Don't you realize that every soul has its share of
predicaments, all of which require us to dig deep down
inside to come up with at least a shimmer of hope?
That takes might.

Strength is what gets us through perilous times
and helps us to exit practically unscathed. Strength is
what permits our faith to go unquestioned by those
who closely watch us from the sideline. Strength is the

essence of our willpower. Strength is what enables us to resist the pressure from our peers. Strength is what's required to overcome the stress caused by uncontrollable, negative elements. Strength is what we need to create plausible resolutions. Strength is having the decency to admit when you are wrong, without feeling a need to create an excuse. Strength is possessing the ability to continue being generous, despite the selfishness of ungracious wolves. Beware. It takes a different type of strength to avoid those who are toxic by nature.

To make progress takes strength. Not once have you read about things being easy. If we practice becoming an example for others to follow, things will become much smoother, but for now, it would serve us well to remember what it feels like to struggle a bit. Without strength, there is no resilience. Without resilience, there are no internal cries for you to hold on through the tough times, knowing with certainty that something tremendously rewarding is in the making.

Strength is realizing you need to do better, but that in doing so, you must have the discipline and the willpower to overcome what seems to be a never-ending process.

Don't ever indulge in your weaknesses, but think and project strength so you may one day be proud of yourself when your actions display the fortitude of your character.

 **JEWEL**

Always permit the strength of your mind to be projected through your actions.

Ingredients for Creating a Well-Nourished Relationship

> There are people who will say they are
> my friends; but I will say they are only
> associates, others will profess to be my
> family, but I confess that I only consider
> them relatives. Forgive me for I mean
> no insult or harm, and understand
> that I am a man who is aware that
> even Jesus was betrayed by Judas ...
>
> **—FRANK C. MATHEWS**

EVERY RELATIONSHIP WE assist in creating is unique in its own way. Some much more significant than others, but all are equally worth cherishing forever.

Beautiful relationships take time to construct. This is why delicate hands are required to gently instill an appropriate balance of harmony, unforgettable virtues, and a touch of forbearance inside the mortar of every human foundation. It's like a fine cognac whose ingredients are comprised of lots of love, mutual respect, endearing communication, loyalty, honesty, and a tablespoon of patience. Of course, it's an acquired taste. This is what makes it so tasteful. How could something so splendid go unadorned?

Time and dedication are both essential for building an enduring relationship. Only through time, will we learn the importance of sharing, the depths of unquestionable concern for others' feelings, a passion for listening with an eagerness to understand the things that aren't so obvious, and the comfort of a gentle touch on your back to serve as a reminder that you are never alone.

Dedication is entwined with time in order to display admirable devotion—a devotion that knows no limits. It grants you permission to be generous with every ounce of your affection, while relaxing in total comfort, knowing your unconditional love will never be taken advantage of. It whispers words of assurance that say there shall be no judgements made against your imperfections and that it is perfectly normal for you to be loved, in spite of the fact that you find it so hard to see a valid reason to bypass the pain of your loneliness and your longing to be meaningfully fulfilled by someone who knows the value of sometimes stepping up to be your rock!

What would any relationship be worth without having true meaning? It is virtually impossible to maintain a healthy relationship that is absent the correct nourishment needed for it to thrive with happiness.

Hey! Come down a few notches and get rid of those expectations of changing people for reasons that suit your selfish outlook. We are all different for a perfectly good reason. Do you honestly think you would be able to deal with someone who is emotionally, spiritually, and mentally just like you? Let people shine just as they are. If they feel a pressing need to change, it will happen at a time that is right for them; otherwise, you run the risk of causing that special person to become hurt and/or to outright abandon the relationship due to you trying to be so controlling.

Do not waste your time attempting to forge relationships with those who pretend to love and have your best interests in mind but only when convenient for them. You possess an internal strength that is alluring to those who often struggle to make sense of so many different things all at once. When you have a wonderful heart, you will notice that people, even those who are unpleasant, will gravitate to you and try to find a way to befriend you. They will swear as though, in their hearts it feels as if they have known you for what seems like forever. Resist such flattery. Later down the line, you will come to realize that you were nothing more than a temporary comfort to those people who were, quite frankly, terrified to acknowledge the thought of being emotionally vulnerable. Being emotionally vulnerable is not such a bad thing. It's the games people choose to play at your expense that are so disheartening.

Tend to relationships the same way you would tend to a prize-winning flower garden. It must be cultivated and well developed. The soil will need to be regularly toiled to rid it of unwanted weeds and harmful pests. Care for it with a sincere dedication that will help you to appreciate the growth and beauty of the bloom. Sure, there are different types of relationships, but if you apply the same recipe with a willingness to be generous with the dosage of love that you provide, you cannot go wrong.

Remember this: you receive from a relationship nothing more than what you invest in it. Be authentic. Have the courage to tell the truth. Create an unbreakable line of heart-to-heart conversations, and never, under any circumstances, be afraid to do all of the small things that speak volumes for how much you truly care. Be inquisitive about the events of your loved one's day. Become more of a listener than a speaker. Encourage and support without critiquing or criticizing the things that are sometimes not immediately meant to be understood.

A relationship that consists of a man and woman together as one requires each to have the other's back every single day, without rest. You know how important it is to choose wisely. There's absolutely no reason why you should choose a life partner who refuses to find pleasure in complementing your thoughts, your strengths, your independence, your abilities, your personal struggles, your innumerable sacrifices, or your belief in yourself, without preconditions.

Relationships aren't supposed to be one-sided, and money isn't everything to a person who is already internally rich. What about you? Are you ambitious, intelligent, responsible, neat, compassionate, an excellent listener, reliable, a go-getter, and God fearing? No, it's not a tall order. It's the science that lies behind the making of your other half.

If you're unable to agree on certain things, try to compromise. The coffee, the cooking, and even the baking may not be all that great. It shouldn't be a major factor. Men, learn to keep your mouths closed and act as if it's the best you have ever had. Show gratitude with true appreciation. Someone thought you were special enough to make time and preparations to cater to you when she could have utilized the moment for doing something more pressing for herself. If you truly want to be of help, suggest the two of you sign up for cooking classes. This is what unconditional love, initiative, and a lasting vision for a valuable relationship looks like. Being discontent with a certain aspect of your relationship does not provide you with a reason to complain about it. It offers you an opportunity to suggest a way of fixing it!

All of our relationships should have eternal value to them, a value of happiness and assistance in growth that's consistent with you evolving mentally, spiritually, and wholesomely.

Create relationships that will contribute to your maturation, as opposed to smother your energy, which will ultimately bring you down to a level of depression.

 **JEWEL**

Strive to make all of
your relationships
smell as pleasant as
the scent of a tulip.

—MS. CURTISE JOHNSON

Accepting
Constructive Criticism

....

A wise son heareth his father's
instructions, but a scorner
heareth not rebuke.

—PROVERBS 13:1

....

NO PERSON WALKING God's green earth was born perfect. We all have had some type of character defect at one time or another. It doesn't matter if there's one or two; they are flaws nonetheless, requiring immediate correction due to the destructive potential they can have on us, as well as on those who have our best interests in mind.

Accepting constructive criticism can be very difficult sometimes. Understand, it is not an opportunity to annoy you or cause you to feel belittled in front of your peers. It is supposed to be a moment to persuade you to honestly evaluate your shortcomings from the perspective of someone who appreciates you enough to let you know when you are acting less than admirable.

Contemplation, as it pertains to accepting feedback

on your inadequacies, will take strength and discipline. Not everyone can accept the fact that their character is not as good as they would like to believe. Constructive criticism is given to us in hopes that we have the might and common sense to recognize our blemishes and feel a sincere need to make the necessary changes before it becomes too late. Think about it. What real chance would any of us have at becoming the best we can be in life if there was no one who cared enough about us to pull our coat when we displayed distasteful behavior? What can be said of the person who felt concerned enough to pull you aside and admonish you for your constant need to bend the truth? It seems we've come to love a distorted truth because, in our moments of sickness, it permits us to emphatically believe there is absolutely nothing wrong with blaming others for our mistakes.

No one who has an ounce of concern for you will ever say anything with the intention of trying to embarrass you. The world is full of great people who are experienced, wise, and know a thing or two about enhancing the potential of others. Find the humility to quietly listen when someone is trying to show you an error in your ways.

Learn to appreciate the difference between a person who finds an unwarranted need to criticize everything you do and a person who is trying to enrich your character through gently showing you, not only what you're doing or saying that is wrong, but how to do it a little more appropriately.

Do not be like those who are quick to judge and criticize others without recognizing the need to take a deep look inside of themselves first.

....

It is always easy to enjoy a laugh
at the expense of another person's
follies, but the humor quickly
turns sour when the mistake has
been found to be your own.

—WILLIAM BREEDEN

....

Take your time when correcting the things that aren't so great about yourself. Being able to accept constructive criticism is what will help you to become golden. We work on ourselves one step at a time. The clock will favor you as long as you are not attempting to milk it with unwarranted excuses and delays.

There will be times when you won't be able to pick up on the purpose of criticism from those who despise you for reasons they themselves remain oblivious to. Don't allow it to deter you. Everyone has something you can learn from, even a buffoon. When constructive criticism is offered to you, try your best to pay close attention with detached emotions. Upon reflection, if it proves to have validity, make the necessary adjustments, but should what they say prove to be worthless, just smile, knowing that your critic may secretly resent everything about your whole style.

Having genius in your DNA does not preclude you from needing to know all there is to know about how to move and how to speak. We must never become combative or arrogant towards those who are trying to show us a better way to mature.

> If you do not accept criticism
> you must look after yourself.
>
> **—TSONGA PROVERB**

There will come a time when the truth may sting a bit, but comfort can be found in realizing we are surrounded by people who truly have our backs. Value and embrace what those who care about you have to offer. In the offered wisdom can be found something that may assist you in becoming a better person. Stop being overly sensitive all of the time by thinking every criticism extended to you is meant to be an insult. In an attempt to help us elevate from one level of consciousness to another, it is essential for those who say they care about us to remember to offer a touch of praise when we are doing well.

What would school be like without a teacher who provides instructions to ensure that we have a better chance to not only comprehend correctly, but be ready to advance to the next level? If it is your aspiration to become the best, you must be willing to acknowledge your deficiencies so they do not become habitual.

> It is difficult to criticize someone
> who makes conscious decisions
> and constantly strives to act
> in a responsible manner.
>
> **—DERRICK SMITH**

If you want to become a wise student of life, you must be able to accept criticism, even when it comes from those you may not be so fond of. Do not waste your time worrying about what others are doing wrong. Make sure the road you are traveling is free of rubbish that could hinder your progress.

J E W E L

There is only one way to avoid criticism: Do nothing, say nothing, and be nothing.

— ARISTOTLE

True Appreciation Leaves a Warm Feeling with Others

....

Making one person smile can
change the world—maybe not the
whole world, but their world.

—ANONYMOUS

....

S **HOWING THE DEPTHS** of our gratitude
for the generosity bestowed upon us by others
is a hallmark of having an enriched character.
Those who make time to do things for us need
to know how appreciated they really are. No, not
because they seek to have their deeds acknowledged,
but because it may serve as a form of healing to a
wounded soul. Once such an act has been established,
they will be much more confident knowing that when
an occasion arises, you will be more than willing to
pay a similar deed forward to another person. There
is nothing like witnessing a warm smile on someone's
face because you showered them with the sincerest
affection from the depths of your heart.

Be mindful: any complaints lodged by you pertaining to the manner in which people have done things for you or how little they may have given you will only serve to highlight your ungratefulness. It becomes a sad day on earth when we allow our personal conduct to deteriorate to a point where we become unable to recognize when appreciation is warranted. Count your many blessings and be grateful you have someone who cares enough to do things on your behalf. Being thankful can be infectious.

When we forget our manners, it's the surest way to leave distaste in the hearts of others. The last thing you should ever want is to have a loved one contemplating regret for thinking you were worthy of his/her time and effort to bring a touch of joy to your life.

Every day we all can find at least one thing to be appreciative for, even if it's only an appreciation for being blessed to have awakened to see another day. What could be more gratifying than that? You are alive! Is it impossible for you to realize how many people missed out on the gift of life today? No matter what your state of mind is, you are blessed, and all that remains is for you to make sure others know how thankful you really are.

 **JEWEL**

Give others a chance to enjoy the warm feeling of being appreciated.

—SHAMIAH STARLING

Actions Are More Pleasing than Words

....

Beware of irresolution of thy
actions, beware of instability in the
execution; so shalt thou triumph over
two great failings of thy nature.

–KEMETIC PROVERB

....

WORDS HAVE NO value without actions
to provide them with substance. We have
become accustomed to hearing people do
entirely too much talking about this and that, without
having been afforded the opportunity to witness their
promises being transformed into actions.

Being an excellent listener with an ability to comprehend is meaningless when you don't possess wisdom
or a strong desire to get things done. The cause you
champion must be greater than yourself. Your actions
will have an impact on core issues relating to the refinement of humanity.

....

If you do not fight for something
important for the greater good,
you will waste your life away on
everything that is insignificant.

–LARRY GREGORY

....

Nelson Mandela (1918–2013) spent twenty-seven agonizing years in prison for embarking upon the seemingly endless journey of fighting to end apartheid in South Africa. He was truly the epitome of what a thinker with courage looks like. Selfless in every step he took, from the first day of his mission.

....

Hard work signifies persistence
and patience. To achieve great
accomplishments, we must
have a hardworking spirit.

–SHIH CHENG YEN

....

After an extensive, oppressive wait in prison, he was set free through a negotiated deal. His name was placed on the ballot and he went on to become South Africa's first democratically elected president.

Apartheid was a brutal legalized system comprised of the highest forms of racism and deprivation. It was a nasty strategy that was utilized to segregate and viciously discriminate against people solely because of the color of their skin. Can you even imagine what it was like to struggle and suffer on a daily basis while agonizing over the question of how one could endure such extremities yet continue to embrace the dignity of being a human?

How humiliating it must have been to feel as though you were inferior to everyone, other than those who courageously struggled alongside of you. This came at a time when most people weren't convinced they had God-given rights. How could they? Apparently, the government's only objective was to instill fear in folks every single day! They were kicked, stomped, and beat mercilessly with truncheons for no apparent reason, on sight.

Nelson Mandela's courageous actions will forever serve as an example worth emulating. A true hero; someone who was unapologetic for what he felt in his heart and for what needed to be done on behalf of millions of South Africans when they weren't convinced they could do it for themselves.

When you have the courage to engage in a life-altering cause, the more you do to help advance the convictions of others, the more favorable you'll become as a legitimate agent for truth and justice for everyone.

Do not think it is sufficient to only listen with your ears. We must learn to listen with our hearts as well. Pay attention to what people do and let it resonate deep within. Thus, you will learn not only the true character of people, but how passionate they are about their deeds and the causes they are so fond of.

Our actions are a manifestation of the thoughts that we occupy. Create thoughts that will focus on solutions and be in front as an example and inspiration for all.

....

If you fight with your tongue
only, you lose the battle.

—AKAN PROVERB

Strive to become a man or woman
whose actions are more beautiful
than the articulation of their words.

—CLARENCE CUMMINGS

....

When our actions can be looked upon as having established the standard for a cause, it becomes incumbent upon us to become a beacon of that criterion. Nothing more, and certainly nothing less, will be expected of you. Make sure you always complete what you have begun. The end result will be a direct reflection of your restless dedication and an earned credit to your character.

Try to be cognizant of the things going on around you so you don't become a victim of others' unthoughtful actions. Every person thinks and acts differently. Some are razor-sharp, while others will never be anything more than a butter knife. When you are trying to perfect the smaller things, take your time and think. Sooner or later, you will acquire a reliable moral compass that can help ensure all of your actions have been executed in a tasteful manner.

The average person's actions are performed in haste. Sloppiness of some degree is usually the end result. The mentality of folks with such an attitude is filled with schemes that are meant to serve their self-interest. Be wiser than that.

Don't be a half-stepper. Embark upon no task with the intent of doing it only halfway. There are no short-cuts when your actions are for the purpose of creating a lasting change. Work your hardest and be certain that you've done your best.

Everything we do in life should be a reflection of our righteousness, as well as an opportunity to bring justice to those who have known injustice far too long. What are we talking about? We are discussing how important it is for you to persevere when things become extremely difficult and you find yourself scratching your head wondering, "What am I doing here?" It's rather simple. You are striving to make sure your actions bring comfort to someone other than yourself, even when your intent is aimed at accomplishing personal goals. Our actions should always be worth at least a warm smile to the onlookers.

 **JEWEL**

Those who truly know a few things could care less about what you're saying; they would rather see your actions speak.

—DARYL BUTLER

Give Advice in Small Doses

IN OUR MOMENTS of uncertainty, receiving the right kind of advice from the right people is important. Whether we find ourselves cautiously dispensing it to those who value our opinion or have the pleasure of being the recipients, it is incumbent upon us all to, not only be excellent listeners, but to be someone who provides advice in small doses.

As much as we would love to believe that we are the professors of some prestigious university, it just isn't so. Check your credentials and learn to appreciate your role.

Intelligent people from all walks of life graciously humble themselves when seeking trusted counsel. What gives us the audacity to think it's okay to inject our opinions and advice in matters we know very little about? Sometimes you have to be as smooth as the wise owl who sits undetected in the tree, intently watching everything moving about below.

Having the insight to recognize when to offer your advice conveys that you're also mature enough to comprehend the suggestions of those who know a bit more than you. Don't be so quick to speak; just listen. Not all wise men and women speak a lot. When the moment is ripe, your advice will be sought.

> A novice should never
> feel emboldened to offer
> guidance to her teacher.
> **— DONALD BROWN**

Try not to be so overconfident in your advice to others as to make the mistake of a fool by attempting to impart the words of a counselor upon those who clearly possess more knowledge than you.

Solid advice from the wise will unquestionably make your journey not only more comfortable, but much easier to travel.

JEWEL

Seek the advice of wise
counsel when you are
in doubt and some day
someone may choose
to ingratiate themselves
with your advice.

—DAVID CHRISTINA

Every Heart
Should Know the
Delicateness
of Empathy

A heart that is devoid of empathy will
never be permitted to experience the
true passions of love, the excitement
of happiness nor the solidarity
of an enduring relationship.

—TIM BUTTLER

WE HAVE ALL been created with a heart
of compassion, a mind with remarkable
depth, and a resounding soul that was once
more pleasing than the scent of lilacs. Where did we
go wrong?

Both as youths and adults, someplace along the
way, we have suffered psychological, physical, and emotional abuse. In such fragmented moments, our ability
to be empathetic was lost.

For those of us who have never known such

traumatizing circumstances, we possess the ability to wear the pain of others, no matter how heartrending the expression of their agony may be.

Empathy is patiently listening as a person confides in you the torments of his/her suffering, whether it's a looming possibility or actual loss. Even though it is virtually impossible to fully understand exactly how someone who has lost a piece of himself/herself may feel unless you have gone through a similar experience, your ability to visualize and sympathize as if you have suffered personally proves you are capable of being empathetic.

Perhaps listening to someone relive the worst day of his/her life, may cause you to shed tears. Stepping into the shoes of another is empathy. It doesn't make you less of a man or woman because you allow others to see you emotionally vulnerable. This is the way to become a better individual. Whatever you may have gained from living vicariously through the pain of another, even if only for a single day, remember, that person's life has been altered forever, and he/she will never be the same again.

Have you ever watched a movie that caused you to become emotional? It's okay. It is nothing more than the validation of your soul having an abundance of empathy. Always try to understand the source of someone else's pain: the person's loss, as well as the violations he/she has suffered at the hands of someone who was wicked at heart. You are not the only person who has gone through something unforgettable.

Allow others' sadness to serve as a reminder to you that it is better to be of service to others than it is to be the person whose actions create pain for so many who are undeserving.

 **JEWEL**

Don't be afraid to show the world that you have a heart.

–PALOMA SALCIDO

Weakness Is
Easily Detectable

....

The scent of weakness is
enough to repulse any decent
person from taking interest.

–GLENN BRANCALEONI

....

LET THE STRENGTH of your character be exemplified in all you say and do. Do not become an example of weakness. In doing so, you risk being marked for life. A determination to seek true justice with power that has the potential to benefit the righteous should be enough to prevent you from being ensnared by the traits of a weak individual. You are courageous, not a quitter.

Let it be a disciplined anger that awakens your consciousness, propelling you to help transform the less informed into something more dignified.

Those who are weak must be led. They constantly have to be told what to do and how to do it. Where's the strength in that? Those who are broken-down are without vision, self-respect, tenacity, or a dash of hope. They will be quick to tell you, "It is what it is!" You should detest those who show weakness without having an inclination to become stronger. There is absolutely no reason why anyone should not have a valuable opinion of their self-worth. We are an image of God; how grateful we should be. In fact, what more can we ask for?

Being weak in mind will not allow our personal elevator to go any higher than the first level of an underground garage. It will prevent us from entertaining the possibility of acquiring additional knowledge that can show us how to fix what is inadequate within us.

Our debilitating thoughts have never inspired us to seek much, and due to having such a lack of motivation, we remain at the bottom, full of complaints. A weak person is like a tumor. It must be surgically removed to prevent it from spreading.

If you are weak in mind, you will be weak in your heart, and if you are weak in your heart, your character will never be able to prosper.

Fear and weakness are foes of self-confidence. It is highly unlikely that you will find weakness of character existing in a person who has a healthy mind, unless it is a ruse. When we can envision greatness and realize the potential of our capabilities, weakness will franticly search for a new host. Why do you claim it is okay to be a cringing, weak-minded individual? You're afraid to ascend the unknown! God would never provide us with the words needed to articulate such a pitiful excuse. Our dignity shouldn't allow us to either.

 **J E W E L**

There's no excuse for being weak.

Ignorance Is a Preventable Disease

....
The ignorant praises his own ignorance.

—SWAHILI PROVERB
....

I **T HAS BEEN** said, "Ignorance is bliss." A consideration of such a sentiment seems to be valid. What conceivable rationale could be offered for attempting to elaborate on things that we have no knowledge of?

I mean, when we come upon an object that is unknown to us, our natural curiosity should pose the question, "What is it?" It can be very difficult when no one is able to help provide an answer, and in our moment of uncertainty, we attempt to guess what a thing is. This is a huge error in our logic. It's not plausible to speculate.

I am bound to inform you that there is absolutely no harm in admitting you do not know, unless you choose to be known as a fool. It's quite simple. When you do not know something, just say, "I don't know the answer." There is rarely a penalty for acknowledging that you do not know certain things. However, there is much respect that stands to be gained when you possess the courage to express a willingness to find out. This is one of the reasons why it's so important to study and surround yourself with folks who know a few things. After you have done your homework and consulted with people who are knowledgeable, if you are still unable to solve your problem, do more research and ask more questions. Continue to search for an answer and you will find one. This is what happens when you are persistent.

Now you can see why education is so important. Don't ever give up. Keep searching until you are able to definitively understand what you are trying to figure out. Have the curiosity of a kid. You know kids ask an assortment of questions, and so should you! If you don't ask, you will never know.

Ignorance stems from you failing to think your way through challenging problems. When people think, it pays off. Would you like to know what becomes of those who fail to correctly utilize their power of thought? They remain ignorant and squander away a perfectly good opportunity to leave their mark on the world.

Do not provide anyone with a reason to call you ignorant! Those who could care less find themselves at the bottom of life, subjected to ridicule and the title of a fool. Learn to think your way through your difficulties.

 **JEWEL**

Ignorance can destroy your chance to someday be great.

There's No Need
To Be Greedy

....

The person who eats larger helpings
does not care that there is a famine.

—YORUBA PROVERB

....

WHAT SHALL BE spoken of the greedy
spirit that finds distaste in unselfishly
sharing with others? A spirit that has failed
to extend the slightest hint of an apology for being nig-
gardly, materialistic, and meager in substance? Please,
quickly turnaround and walk the other way while
the moment is timely. For the tale of such despicable
conduct is not something you should ever want to be
associated with.

Many deformities of the heart can be found cloaked
in greed, beginning with a consistent discontent for what
one has been blessed to enjoy. Sadly, it carries a weight
that means very little to those who are ungrateful of
being in a position to provide so much.

Greed has been found to be an indispensable necessity for those who have a covetous appetite. It does not

discriminate. Everyone, despite the color of their skin or social standings, is a potential victim of its selfish ways. It has no concern for what the well-being and contentment of another's heart may be like. If only it had the empathy and compassion to refrain from taking more than its allotted share. I know, wishful thinking.

The poisonous tentacles of greed have the ability to subtly infect the fainthearted with jealousy and pettiness, if such a contagious disease is not already a condition of the soul.

How will jealousy appear? Folks will act indifferent towards you. "No" will be a relished answer to any favor you request or humanity that you may be seeking from those who have more than enough to go around.

Pettiness reveals its rotten face when profuse contemplation is given to what may remain after a portion has been reluctantly dispensed. Allow me to share something of great importance with you: a person whose heart is not consumed with greed will never be fretful about what the remainder of *anything* might be, once he/she has extended a hand to someone who may need just a little bit more.

Those of us who are internally wealthy have been blessed with a beautiful heart that will assist in obtaining so much more than what we are capable of physically seeing, but not until the time is appropriate.

Under no circumstance should you ever feel a need to be greedy. The gluttonous discomfort you cause others to endure will one day return to deceitfully smother you. It will be nothing more than the consequence of your pretentious ignorance.

 **JEWEL**

An illiberal spirit wants
nothing more than to
deny you the pleasure
of enjoying the virtue
of sharing with those
who are kindhearted.

—EARL SMITH

The Story of Time

....

Nine-tenths of wisdom consists
in being wise in time.

–THEODORE ROOSEVELT

....

THE SUN IS the gatekeeper of duration. From it we accept its sustenance and have learned to depend on it as an accurate implement for measuring what we can never get enough of: time.

Due to life extending to us no more than a brief moment to bask in its grace, and life's loyal companion, time, being unrelenting in its determination to never stand still for anyone, there exists an implication that our time is more valuable than we tend to realize. So many miss its beauty. Fewer pray for more. Learn to use it correctly and you will enjoy what it has in store. Be appreciative and it will show you generosity. Abuse it and you will forever be filled with regrets.

Most of us mismanage our time and never find the happiness life has to offer. For the stable person, time is a blessing, but for the mentally unbalanced, it can be a nuisance. Relax a little. Learn what it takes to be an agent of time.

Choose your appointments with precision. Carefully select those you wish to bless with your time, at a moment that is feasible for you, and not a second before. Show the world how much you value your seconds, minutes, hours, and the preciousness of your allotted days. After all, if you are foolish enough to allow others to waste your precious gift, you only have yourself to be upset with.

Anything that is worth something takes time to mature. Someone believes in you, and so it is only right for you to believe in yourself. Hard work takes time before its labor can be enjoyed. The fruit from a tree takes time to mature. Healthy relationships take time to properly establish. No, it will not happen overnight, but things are in your favor. There is no reason why you are not salvageable. Time offers mercy in favor of your correction now, but you must want it bad enough. Why? Well, because:

....

Men are not philosophers, but are rather very foolish children who by reason of their partiality see everything in the most absurd manner, and are victims at all times of the nearest object.

—RALPH WALDO EMERSON

....

Someone thinks you are special enough to be given the ingredients for nourished growth—it doesn't matter who. Recognize the value of your time and take full advantage of every opportunity. There is an appropriate occasion for everything. Be diligent at all costs.

Please, don't misuse your allotted time chasing after things that have no significance. It is offensive to your spirit, as well as to those who have the utmost concern for you as a human being.

JEWEL

Never mimic the shadow who is constantly in pursuit of the sun.

What Have You Been Through if You Don't Know What it Means to Struggle or Suffer?

True courage is knowing how to suffer.

—HAITIAN PROVERB

NO PERSON WHO has gone through something significant ever says that life and the development of the mind and character comes easily and without knowing what it means to struggle. How can we possibly come to understand our inner strengths if we have never collided head-on with any type of adversity?

Struggling is nothing new. Many folks have struggled and suffered in some of the worst ways imaginable. It is a universal fact that if struggling is patiently endured, it can help create humility, gratitude, compassion, and great fortitude. There are very few amongst us who have not experienced some type of suffering or emotional trauma that has left us heartbroken and struggling for a very long time. Life's paths will be littered with difficulties of various magnitudes and tales of suffering that exist solely to either challenge our resolve or crush our spirit.

Precious jewels aren't extracted from mines already looking illustrious. Rocks have the potential to be beautiful, no matter how unimpressive they initially appear to be, but first they have to be pressured and beat up before they can be considered worthy of being a jewel. Think about it. If stones have to violently collide and tumble against each other and be ground against abrasives before we can see their luster, who are we to prematurely expect to shine before experiencing the stress of struggling?

We go through trials, tribulations, losses, and sufferings in hopes of giving God a reason to be proud of us when we don't forget to call upon him in our moments of difficulty. We are never alone. God is ever watchful and so nonjudgmental. All that is required of us is to maintain our faith. Should we begin to falter, we must tap into our inner strength.

....
Birds flying against the wind
are the strongest. Those flying
with it are the weakest.
—AFRICAN WISDOM
....

Pick your head up and continue pressing forward.

Struggling isn't something that should make you bitter. Smile while nurturing the thought of things becoming better. No deplorable conditions last forever. Knowing the things you know should provide you with great confidence and certainty that it's only a matter of time before the tides change in your favor. You must find the ability to look well beyond your troubles and whatever obstacle that may be in your way so you can see the sun that is shining on the other side!

What no one seems to have mentioned to us is the fact that struggling and suffering purify the soul. It's evident Mother Nature multiplies through purification of her own kind. Wake up and see things for what they are. When a seed dies, new life comes into existence. There are numerous flowers that will not produce a fragrance unless they are smashed, snapped, crushed, or in some way bruised. Yes, it is a different form of suffering. One that slightly differs in comparison to how we identify with suffering on a human level.

It is a well-known fact that diamonds cannot be created without extreme heat and pressure from the earth. Again, this is another form of struggling. Human beings aren't the only entities that have to be tested by way of struggles and suffering.

Arguably, no man except Isa (Jesus) has ever suffered more that Ayyub (Job) did in a single lifetime. While in the midst of his greatest suffering, Job cried, "When he hath tried me, I shall come forth as gold," (Job 23:10). In spite of all the things he had gone through, he was still able to understand that God continued to guide him, working miraculous wonders in his life. God never, not even for a second, deserted Job during his times of struggling.

See, when we are unafraid to struggle, that's when

we experience some of the most priceless lessons of life. Then we will begin to gradually understand that life is about so much more than what we expect. It becomes easier to follow our desire to counsel and guide others out of the wilderness. Only when we are truly ready to embrace such humility will we be able to ease the deep-rooted pain of our past sufferings.

Possessing such compassion for others will unquestionably find its way back to your doorstep. There will come a time when your help is needed because you have been through troubled waters and you know all too well what struggling and suffering is about. How can anyone be confident when verbally sharing with you if you have never been through anything significant?

You shouldn't be ashamed to admit that your experiences can attest to the pain you've encountered while struggling a little more than others. It doesn't make you less of a person. If anything, it makes you a stronger individual. Deep down inside of us all there is a vibrant soul waiting to be discovered, if we can prove that we have been able to survive the humiliation of life's hardships.

When we attempt to escape adversity, it makes us fragile. It casts us in a light of having a false sense of entitlement with thoughts of being better than others. Through struggling, opportunities arise for us to see who shall emerge resiliently and shine brightly with a sincere smile of indebtedness.

> Iron is passed through
> fire to be hardened.
>
> **—SWAHILI PROVERB**

> Every struggle, whether won or
> lost, strengthens us for the next to
> come. It is not good for people to
> have an easy life. They become weak
> and inefficient when they cease
> to struggle. Some need a series of
> defeats before developing strength
> and courage to win a victory.
>
> **−VICTORIO (OF THE CHEYENNE)**

Some of us have been through so much, while others have gone through absolutely nothing at all.

> You have wisdom, but you haven't
> suffered; who is your teacher?
>
> **−YORUBA PROVERB**

Take a look at how mentally attractive you are now. You have become a consciously dignified, responsible survivor of past unconscionable acts. Now you too may tell your story with confidence.

Struggling and suffering shouldn't cause you to feel embarrassed, nor should they leave you feeling humiliated. It's a valuable experience that does all good-hearted people justice in the end. Who will ever know if you don't possess the courage to convey your story of horrific events?

....

He who lies by the fire
knows how it burns.

—AFRICAN PROVERB

....

When our humility prevents us from forgetting those countless nights of suffering and struggling, we will be more cautious of where and with whom we walk.

 **J E W E L**

Do not be afraid to struggle. It can do nothing but help you to become a better person.

Blessings Are All Around Us!

One ought, each day at least, to hear
a little song, read a good poem,
see a fine picture and, if possible,
speak a few reasonable words.

—GOETHE

NO MATTER HOW young or how ripe you are, we all receive our personal share of blessings. Now, whether or not you possess the humility to recognize them is a different tale to be told.

Every day that we are given an opportunity to witness another sunrise is a blessing that should be welcomed with nothing less than gratitude. Forget complaining about what you may not have. Smile and eagerly rejoice in the blessing for what has been provided for you.

Make time to explore the beauty around you. You have health, your sanity, and a heart filled with compassion. It doesn't matter that you are without materialistic objects that appeal to your ego or contribute to your misconceived status. Be thankful for the many blessings that have been tailor-made just for you. It is those who act as if they are incapable of recognizing and appreciating their blessings who will most likely never know what it means to be blessed on a grand scale.

Entirely too much time is wasted worrying about what other people have or what they are doing, or wishing you were blessed to be in their shoes. That's a problem we have all faced at some point in life. Because we have yet to learn how to be grateful for the smaller things we already have, our spirits have not been blessed to receive the larger things that are conceivable.

Most of us can relate to what it means to be down and out. You know, when things seem to be unendingly gloomy and stressful. The healing water that is supposed to be clear with revitalizing inspiration is somehow nothing other than murky and deplete of serenity. Fortunately, some of us have family and friends who've chosen to endure turbulent times with us. Sacrificing, giving, counseling, and protecting. How blessed we are! Don't forget to pay homage to those who stuck by your side when you were at rock bottom. The people you see on your way up will be the same folks you see on your descent. Nobody lives on top forever.

If the blessings you receive in life cause you to be elevated, do not forget to take the people who were with you from the beginning along for the eventful journey.

Blessings sometimes come camouflaged in different disguises. The more you do for others from the genuineness of your heart, the more abundant will be your blessings. They will never appear when we want them to, but rest assured, they will come, as everything in the universe has its moment.

None of us has everything we want, but we all have something special, and for that blessing alone we must learn to be tremendously thankful.

Our blessings are custom-made for each of us. Play your part in life! Blessings will not always be transparent. Sometimes they will appear while you're in the midst of adversity. Life requires all of us to go through difficulties of some type in order to receive what has been cleverly put off to the side. At the end, we have a chance to gain a double reward: one, we are given the gift of blessings, and two, we gain the experience of a valuable lesson that can be utilized to help someone else in need. Maintain a giving heart and you will never be without a spirit that is equipped to receive.

J E W E L

It is a blessing to be able to read and comprehend.

The Richness of Elders

....

If there is any philosophy, it's that
those who have walked a certain path
should know some things, should
remember some things that they
can pass on, that others can also
use to walk the path a little better.

—ELLA BAKER

....

ELDERS ARE THE face of strength, the spirit of ambition, and a tremendous comfort to those of us who are nothing more than misunderstood. There should never exist a single moment without a show of respect for older people. The act itself seems to have become a lost practice. Certainly, they are worth paying homage to. They are human repositories of mental jewels and advice filled with ascending instructions.

I wouldn't dare attempt to infringe on your personal beliefs, but I must remind you that after children, our elders are the most angelic inhabitants of the earth.

Works of exquisiteness. God's finest! It has been said, "Experience is the best teacher," and because elders' experiences, journeys, and truths surpass ours, respect is mandatory. Sure, we possess spontaneity spiced up with youthful energy, but older people have wisdom and proficiency that we can only pray to someday attain. Besides, who else could possibly qualify for being the epitome of the alluring values we impatiently try to obtain? Respect the waiting line. There are people in front of you for a reason. An elder would love nothing more than to sit in comfort while sharing wisdom with those of us who will cherish, respect, and protect what he/she bestows upon us. Despite what some may say, elderly people are not ill-tempered or unapproachable. It's pain that they feel. When you consider the fact that they have paved the way for us to safely arrive in comfort, it shouldn't be hard to understand why they think we consider them to be disillusioned, irrelevant, and out of touch with reality. Truthfully, maybe we should take a look at ourselves before being so judgmental.

Try listening more. We have a way of turning them off because we talk entirely too much, when we should be listening with patience and a display of appreciation. These are the people who not only possess knowledge capable of purifying our minds; they also possess knowledge that can be utilized to advance our positions in life. In return, all they ask for is respect, honesty, gratitude, and a promise to pass the lesson on to someone who may be worthy. How sweet is that?

The friendship of an elder is full of love and endurance. To sustain it, we must be authentically wise in our dealings. Be smart. When someone helps you become a better person, you owe it to that person to move with class. Older people know all too well the characteristics of a golden soul, but who in their right mind would want to impart knowledge upon someone who pretends to know everything but really knows nothing at all? Elders are seers, and we are nothing more than wondering seekers. How could you be foolish enough to think you can outwit God's most loyal soldiers? Do not take my word as gold; look around and see who occupies the most powerful positions in the world. You don't get there by being foolish.

When you have been invited to sit amongst elders, remember to leave behind your ego, false pride, and that displeasing chip on your shoulder! They won't always look you directly in the eye—unless you have royally screwed up. Pay close attention and be courteous. This is your moment to absorb something extremely valuable. Upon departing, do not forget to say thank you. Always show respect and sincere gratitude, and maybe, just maybe, you may be welcome to return.

Occasionally, offer a gift to serve as a token of your appreciation. They love us and will always have our best interests at heart. All we have to do is act like we have a little sense. That isn't too much to ask, is it? Life would not be so fulfilling without their guidance. Who could ever replace the love of your grandparents? Priceless, right?

For every experience that older people have endured, there is a valuable lesson to be gained. Translation: They know better than we do. They are the queens and kings, and we are merely pawns in a critical game of chess. Act as if you would be honored for them to show you the way.

 **JEWEL**

The world would be in shambles without the wisdom of our elders.

Beggars Have No Qualms

Be certain to pay for whatever it
is that you want. Don't ever feel
a need to beg for anything.

—DAVID LEE

WHAT HAS CAUSED the moral fabric of people's minds to erode so badly that they find comfort in being beggars? Everyone has an opinion to offer, but no one truly knows the answer. Through truth I have found myself convinced that no man or woman in possession of intelligence and the ability to physically function should ever find himself/herself without the essentials needed to begin a journey.

Being a beggar or someone who has come to expect others to do for you should create a strong distaste deep within. Aside from a free ride, what benefits can be gained from allowing others to do for you what you are perfectly capable of doing for yourself? Don't be so quick to accept handouts before making a sincere attempt to apply yourself.

Learn to have an appreciation for the things you are able to do. Resources are everywhere. You can generate powerful thoughts that will provide you with beautiful ideas that, in turn, can prevent you from ever having to beg. Forget about crying in despair. Do not be counted amongst those who intentionally drown in self-pity. Get up and do something about it. Rejoice in the spirit of prosperity. Forget about living a life full of impulse and instinct. It will only prepare you for hardships and an inability to reap the fruits of wholesome thoughts. There are dire consequences for poor decision making. Don't take my word for it; look around.

Your worth is valuable, unless you are someone who is unable to recognize your contributions. Stand up and create what you want from life.

How can you look anyone in the eyes after begging for assistance, knowing within your heart that you haven't given yourself a sincere chance to succeed?

Maintain your dignity and try even harder to control your desires. Do you not realize there are people in the world waiting for you to come crawling on your hands and knees crying for help? They cannot wait to laugh at the humiliation you have endured, nor will they pass up the opportunity to tell you no when you make a simple request.

Under no circumstances should you find yourself downtrodden with your hands out accepting scraps and conjecture from people who think, in their sick minds, that they are better than you. There is nothing ignorant or unsophisticated about you. Try a little bit harder, that's all. Don't humiliate yourself by being a beggar. If you are to extend your hand, let it be to give. Should you decide to give, be certain that the receivers will appreciate and responsibly utilize the gifts you have bestowed upon them to help improve the voyage of someone else.

JEWEL

Begging creates a stench that is difficult to get rid of.

Do You Have Self-Respect?

When self-respect takes its rightful
place in the psyche, you will not allow
yourself to be manipulated by anyone.

—INDIRA MAHINDRA

IT IS IMPOSSIBLE to have a genuine respect for others if you have no concept of what it means to have respect for yourself.

To have self-respect means to have a reasonable amount of pride in who you are. It means walking with your head up. Dressing in a dignified manner. Not allowing others to walk over you and doing your absolute best. It's having gratitude for how far you've come in developing your principled foundation.

Having true love for yourself will not permit you to seek refuge in wrongful acts or thoughts capable of eroding your moral compass. Self-respect is refraining from violating the integrity of your being in any way. Such transgressions are usually what cause us to find ourselves in compromising positions with overwhelming thoughts that largely consist of wondering how we got there. These are the same thoughts that have been, at some point, entertained by every one of us who has dug a deep hole without having the sense to recognize when enough was enough. If we truly have self-respect, there should be an acknowledged limitation to everything that we do.

Treat yourself well. Maintain positive thoughts. Look presentable. Think before you act, and speak as if you have a touch of class. Do what's right, and prove that you care about others. The world is forever watching your every step and looking for a reason to dim the lights on you.

You know what must be done in order to be respectful to yourself. Anytime we have to contemplate the consequences of our poor behavior, we have shown injustice to our integrity, to our minds, and to our existence. Love yourself the best way that you know how, and some day you will attract something dear to your soul.

 **J E W E L**

Respect for yourself is what helps you to shine like no other.

The Silly Games
People Play

Standards of conduct were just as
rigid as the laws of any other people,
but force was seldom used to enforce
good conduct. Each person was
his own judge. Deceitfulness was
a crime. We lived according to our
own standards and principles, not
for what others might think of us.

—THOMAS WILDCAT ALFORD

WHY DO PEOPLE play mental games at
the expense of others? Games are played
for self-serving purposes that, on the surface, appear to have minimal repercussions; that is,
until someone is physically or emotionally harmed.
Those who play mind games see an opportunity to
be deceitful and pretend as if they have some type of
magical power over others.

When you have yet to mature and life in your eyes
consists of nothing but schemes and deceptive ways to

take advantage of other people, this is when the games begin without any consideration at all for those around us. Now, instead of using your mind to build upon something constructive, you have concocted an idea that permits you to manipulate people. You have gone from thinking about ways to better yourself to being a conniver, and in the undertone of your conniving can be found a sickness of the mind and depravity of the heart.

In the criminal world, mind games are commonly known as mental gymnastics. The term serves as an accurate description for those who eagerly seek the chance to bend and twist your thoughts in a way that conforms to their personal desires.

Never play games with other people's thoughts. You wouldn't appreciate someone violating the sanctuary of your mind, so extend the same courtesy to others. Good people who live by moral and ethical boundaries deal with others on the up and up. They abide by the rules. When you start playing games and testing the limitations of others' genuineness, people will quickly grow weary of you and begin to feel as though you cannot be trusted.

Depending on the magnitude of the violation, the consequences can be minor or undesirably strong. You don't have to play games to get what you want in life. Most of the time, if you prove to be a decent person with a good heart, all you have to do is ask. People will be more than happy to oblige you. Trust, love, and loyalty are values that, if found in a person's character, should be cherished until the end of time.

Staying true to yourself will keep you in honorable standing with people of integrity. Your character becomes more pleasant and certainly easier to embrace if you leave the games out of the equation.

While we are exploring the topic of mind games, it's important to draw attention to the deplorable act of playing "misogynistic sex games." This is for all of the immature males who run around on a daily basis masquerading as men. Power and the value of character can never be determined by how many women you can sexually dishonor or by the number of children you help to create without the slightest willingness to accept responsibility for their welfare.

Thinking you are a "player" is a game that little boys play. It is a game that comes with serious ramifications. Still thinking about yourself and how best to satisfy your impulses and desires, huh? Never mind the psychological and emotional imbalance you've caused young women to experience because you never truly intended to fulfill your promise of doing the right thing. You knew when you spoke your first words to her that you were dishonest at heart and that your intentions consisted of nothing more than seeing how far you could get by playing with her mind and heart. You should be ashamed for showing such great disrespect and shallow disregard to potential queens of the earth!

Ladies, you are not without your share of the blame. You are highly perceptive and very intuitive, more so than men. For that reason alone you have the ability to almost smell the insincerity of guys who step beyond your comfort zone with ill intentions. Without a shadow of doubt, you are able to recognize those who only want to fool around, as opposed to those of us who are striving to be productive and who yearn for a chance to experience the sanctity of a real family, something not many of us have had the pleasure of knowing. You really should begin to think more highly of yourselves. Stop being indecisive. If it's boys you want, there is certainly an abundance of them who are ill-fated because of their refusal to do better.

After you have taken a long, hard look inside of yourselves and decide enough is enough. Go out in search of someone who is strong and sincere. Don't be shy. Demand what you want. Every so often you may stumble across a gem in the ruff, but if you are unwilling to patiently invest your time while the gem transforms to its highest quality, what does that say about the conditions of your mind and heart? Having patience with a love that is full of loyalty is the most important thing. Real men and women do not play head games. They communicate clearly so there is no chance for misunderstandings. Leave the games to those who are falsely convinced that they are able to con their way through life. Only through the steadiness of a direct course can you travel into a meaningful horizon.

JEWEL

Games never last for
long. Even Hollywood
superstars slip up on
their act when the
curtain is drawn.

The Signs of a True Friend

Iron sharpeneth iron; so
a man sharpeneth the
countenance of his friend.

PROVERBS 27:17

IF YOU HAVE been blessed to know at least two wonderfully authentic friends in your lifetime, consider yourself to be fortunate. A true friend is rare, almost nonexistent.

Hold a true friend with
both of your hands.

—AFRICAN PROVERB

Allow me to tell you a thing or two about a true friend. A true friend is someone who is an excellent listener, empathetic, caring, reciprocal, and unhesitatingly willing to be completely honest with you, even in the moments when the truth may hurt your feelings. A friend will never lie to you or betray your trust for any reason whatsoever. A friend will often want more for you than they want for themselves. A friend will never abandon you. A friend will stick by your side through both calm and turbulent times. A friend is someone who has nonjudgmental compassion and true love for you. There's no pretending. They are the ones who give us tough love when people begin to feel as though we've become unapproachable. True friends will never attempt to impose their will on you or try to persuade you to go against your better judgment. "A true friend is family!"

If you consider yourself to be a friend, be certain to honor and protect the value of your friendships. When you are wrong, quickly admit you were out of line and offer a sincere apology. Don't demolish friendships; build them up. Strive to be a friend whose company you can't seem to ever get enough of. Cherish your friends because they are irreplaceable. The maintenance of a good friendship takes work. It can be likened to the gardener who finds delight in toiling in and the cultivation of his/her garden.

Let there never arise a moment when you are charged with an accusation of having divulged a friend's secrets or helped to participate in a scheme that has brought about your friend's demise. Don't let it be said that you were a turncoat who turned your back on a friend when he/she needed you the most. Stick by your friends no matter what the weather looks like. Rainy days never last forever! Provide comfort; don't be the one who takes it away.

Not every person is capable of being a true friend.

With that in mind, you must be careful about who you offer your friendship to. You know the difference between a snake and someone who truly cares about you. Utilize your common sense so as to prevent yourself from being bitten by those who only act as if they are your comrades.

A real friend will never smile in your face and gossip behind your back. You can be confident that a friend will honor your name while in the presence of those who have nothing but discontent for you in their hearts. A true friend won't allow you to have sleepless nights over things that are beyond your control.

When contemplating who is worthy of your friendship, be certain that you do not make the mistake of listening to the opinions of others or judging the book by its cover. Yes, it's possible for the cover to accurately depict what the book is about, but a wise person will open the book and explore it in its entirety before casting judgment. It may turn out to be the best book you have ever had the privilege of reading. Would it interest you to know what type of people make really good friends? People just like us! Those of us who have been through something significantly traumatizing, in one aspect or another. Those of us who know how to love from the core but were forced to reserve our feelings until the right person came along, a person who is capable of embracing and cherishing the gift of *us*. Question: why would you even consider becoming friends with someone who has never been through anything that is difficult to express?

When an exceptional friend comes along, you will feel a gravitational pull towards him/her, and your level of solace will greatly increase. There is an unmistakable communication that takes place between attracted souls.

A real friend has a way of reminding us of how special we are. Somehow, true friends effectively create emotions that revive our ability to assess the value we bring to the world on a daily basis. They are never inconsiderate, but very thoughtful in treating us as they would love to be treated. You won't have to beg for their help when you are in need. Just say the word and they will be there.

Many of us have personalities that are very giving. People with the same spirit of generosity can sometimes cause us to feel an embarrassing sense of modesty because we have become so used to doing for others without being accustomed to others bestowing gifts and acts of generosity upon us. Translation? There are those of us who are simply not used to others doing nice things for us without there being a hidden agenda behind the act. Guess what? We are not the only people God utilizes to bless others. We are only a single tool out of so many. In order for others to receive their blessings, they too must execute the wishes of their hearts with at least the same compassion as you.

Be a friend of value to those who are worthy and try hard to add substance to the lives of others. Should they ever pretend to forget the beauty of your heart, fret not. It is a loss that will haunt them for the rest of their lives. Wise is the person who dwells in the company of sincere companions.

 **JEWEL**

True friends are priceless!

A Journey with God

There is one God looking down
on us. We are all children of one
God. God is listening to me. The
son, the darkness, the winds are all
listening to what we now say.

–GOYATHLAY (GERONIMO)

THERE IS A God, and it is in our best interest to recognize how encompassing he is. God is omnipotent. He is the provider of all providers. He is more compassionate than we could ever conceive. He is, without question, the most merciful being and the healer of all hearts and souls.

Never deny God's existence. Through the intelligence of God, men and women have been given life that is full of endless possibilities. Yes, we are made in the image of God, by way of intelligence; however, our intelligence is but a mere speck in comparison to God's wisdom.

No human could ever possess his judiciousness. It is a discernment than can never be questioned for fairness. We are agents of his compassion to the world, placed here for the purpose of making it a better place for all to coexist.

Acknowledge and worship your Lord in every way. For without his blessings, we would have absolutely nothing. Do not allow your ingratitude for being blessed with an opportunity to witness another beautiful day serve as an excuse for why you neglect to give God his just praise. Surely he is more than worthy. It is he who continually provides us with comfort.

Do your best while here on earth. Lose your curiosity for questioning God about his will for things to come. We all receive hardships of different magnitudes to allow us to both examine our resolve and learn what cloth we come from. You cannot change what has been written long before our conception. Have you failed to make time to read the Qur'an, the Torah, or Basic Instructions Before Life Ends (the Bible)? They are truly miraculous books in their own right. The finest that have been revealed to humankind. In them we are continuously reminded that this world is only temporary, and that on any given day, at any hour, minute, or second, we can cease to exist without so much as a warning!

God is all knowing. The best of deliverers. An extraordinary listener whose attention span is beyond any comprehension fathomable to a man or woman. Worship God and only God. That implies never associating him with any partners. How naive we must be to entertain thoughts of him needing help from anyone.

Death is nothing to fear. From God we came and to him we shall someday return. Our physical bodies will be utilized to help replenish the earth, just as the leaves when they fall to the grown after their season's term has expired. Our spirit doesn't abandon the universe. So for what reason do you weep? Death is nothing more than a transformation from one state to another. Consequences? Perhaps it's time to walk correctly.

God is the wisest of all knowers. When we pass away, if our lives have been full of good deeds, as was prescribed for us from the beginning, our souls may have a more realistic chance to be accepted in a higher realm (heaven) and utilized for continuation of a positive usefulness. By God's decree, maybe he will declare us fit for the duties of an angel.

For those who have been evil, malicious, and diabolical in their thoughts and ways, their souls will never be permitted to exist within the universe of prosperity. They will be labeled as outcasts and made to suffer in a way far beyond anything we could ever imagine.

Now do you understand why it is extremely important to do good and execute righteous deeds that help to enhance others? Try to speak of good things and live your life as an example of what good should look like. Worship God and continuously show him your appreciation for his love and numerous blessings, even in the moments when you fall short of remembering the importance of the existence of those blessings. Try to find at least one lost soul and sincerely pray that you may help to alter the course of his/her life for the better.

Congregational prayer is very inspirational, and there are so many blessings to be gained from such a powerful force, but it is your sole duty to worship your Lord and affirm your loyalty to him. No human will be able to intercede on your behalf. We shall all be judged according to our deeds.

It is my personal prayer that something written here will be worthy of serving as inspiration to you and will compel you to make sure that your good deeds outweigh your bad, so at least you may be able to cautiously sit in comfort when the hour of judgment falls upon us.

Please, always place God first. In order to have a balanced life, we must fill our souls with the sincerity of prayer.

 **JEWEL**

When you become lonely, call on God to provide you with discernment.

—LEX BUMPESS

Forgive Those Who Are Truly Sincere

The weak can never
forgive. Forgiveness is the
attribute of the strong.

—MAHATMA GANDHI

OUR STUBBORN INABILITY to forgive those who have wronged us prevents our hearts from reaping the benefits provided by forgiving. Being able to forgive those who seem to effortlessly overlook the pleasantness of our humanity is not about forgetting or ignoring the transgressions committed against us. It's about the restoration of our health, our righteousness, our compassion, and the sanity of our minds.

When we act as if we are unable to forgive, it may cause severe depression and anxiety, two mental diseases that can send us spiraling into despair and misery. Oftentimes, our bitterness quickly transforms to hatred.

Is a failure to forgive others not a conscious error

on our behalf? Aren't we supposed to be engaged in a process of converting our emotional miscalculations into something that is heartwarming and respectable?

You cannot weave your way through life with an attitude that permits you to only accept what appeals to you, while ignoring everything that doesn't. Everything that has been extended to you has been offered in hopes of you being able to correctly learn how to navigate your ship through troubled waters in a manner that is commendable.

The world has more than enough of its share of people who are bitter, discontent, and angry every day. It does not look forward to adding you to the list of those who are overly sensitive and stuck in their ways. You will experience situations in which people who are dear to you wrong you. Naturally, your feelings will be hurt and you may even contemplate refraining from speaking to them. Please reconsider what's at stake. You should not throw away a long-lasting relationship because you lacked not only the foresight and the courage to forgive, but the ability to step into the shoes of another with an understanding of what they may have been going through. Maybe it really was you who was at fault and who initiated the silent treatment.

When we stop speaking to those who care about us, let it be due to a betrayal that cannot be overlooked and not due to a petty misunderstanding. Those who are dear to us deserve to be rewarded with the benefit of the doubt. The first one should always be on you. To discontinue speaking to someone means that, at heart, we consider them to be the equivalent of an enemy. Even forgiving an enemy has value; just be certain not to provide them with anything verbal that may be used to hurt you emotionally! After you have forgiven those who have hurt you, you do not have to immediately force a conversation with them in an attempt to find peace within. Give yourself some time to heal. Let things happen naturally. Think about it. Some of the most alarming deceitfulness requires us to be the bigger person and to create positive ways to step above our emotions.

> If you are unable to forgive a person
> for their infractions, then why should
> anyone forgive you for yours?
>
> **—LEVIN H. MITCHELL**

God forgives us for our wrongs, so what explanation do *we* have for not being able to forgive a mortal who is prone to err?

When someone offends you, immediately bring it to his/her attention. Don't sit and bask in resentment and allow what you're feeling to turn into bitterness. Intelligently verbalize what's on your mind. If the other person is able to truly understand the infraction committed against you and sincerely vows to never allow it to happen again, forgive him/her.

You will not always be spared the vile speech of a drunkard or the conniving tears of a drug addict whom you love dearly. Do not permit the offensive words that stem from his/her addiction to cause you additional pain. Don't be like the person who is quick to anger and constantly in search of justification for why you cannot seem to take the road that leads to forgiveness. Such people believe the world revolves around them, and it's either their way or no way at all. Your mind and soul have no chance for growth and tranquility if you entertain such a selfish disposition.

Here are a few classic excuses we use in the name of not being able to forgive others:

- False pride—"I did the right thing. It wasn't me who decided to cross the line."
- Being overly sensitive—"My heart has been broken one too many times. I just cannot find the strength to forgive and forget."
- Fear—"If I forgive him/her for their transgression, it won't be long before it happens all over again."
- Closed thinking—"I don't want to hear anything that you have to say to me."
- Victim stance—"It was your fault; you said something hurtful to me first."
- Unmanageable anger—"I am entirely too angry to even think about forgiving you right now. I'm going to be honest with you. Forgiving you may never happen."

Do what's right. Go ahead, step beyond the sticking point. Speak up, because in your heart you know you are much better than what you're showing. You cannot help to liberate others if you are unwilling to rid your own heart of the manacles that have been holding you emotionally captive for so long.

It is wise to remember: only those who are fully mature will be able to admit their wrongs and sincerely apologize for their mistakes. Those who are the complete opposite will not be able to admit their errors, and they will swear until their last breath that they have done absolutely nothing wrong. How selfish and irrational they are.

If you've caused someone pain, provide them with space, and when the time is appropriate, go to them offering an apology that comes from the depths of your heart. When you know a thing or two about forgiveness, it means that you do not reside on a one-way street. You don't have the right to ask or expect anyone else to do something you wouldn't do.

We can only show that we have changed through our actions. Before demonstrating the act of change, it is considered befitting to right our wrongs, even if it entails nothing more than sincerely asking to be forgiven. When you have done something wrong, don't wait for others to correct you. Be hasty in scrutinizing your actions and be certain not to allow it to reoccur.

Rectifying our wrongs does not come so easily to everyone. Speak from your heart: "I honestly understand that I have wronged you and my poor decisions have caused you to experience insurmountable pain. I regret my insensitivity. Not only have I sought counseling, but I promise to never again allow my ignorance to supersede my thinking. It is my hope that in due time you may be able to find it in your heart to forgive me." This is fully accepting responsibility for your actions with a sincere request to be forgiven for what may have been the ultimate violation.

Never permit your thoughts to be remiss of this philosophical advice:

....

Sometimes, depending on what
the circumstances are, it can be
much more difficult to forgive
others than it is to muster up the
courage to request forgiveness. Not
all broken hearts mend easily.

—JENNIFER DIXON

....

JEWEL

To sincerely forgive someone takes great strength.

—JOHN BALLARD

Having Consideration for Others

....

> You will find men who want to be
> carried on the shoulders of others,
> who think that the world owes them a
> living. They don't seem to see that we
> must all lift together and pull together.

—HENRY FORD

....

WHAT ADMIRABLE VIRTUES one must possess to be known for having an appreciable gift that reflects upon the needfulness of others way before considering the unassuming desires of themselves. How openhanded is that? Listen not with your ears but with the compassion of your heart, in hopes of discovering a serenade that may be comforting to the souls of others.

What does "having consideration for others" mean? It means being capable of understanding other people's sensitivities. Their plights. Their misfortunes. Their heartaches, both past and present. The value of their time. Their feelings. Their boundaries. Their need to sometimes lean on someone who may be a bit stronger than they are at the moment. It means being able to vicariously step into the shoes of others in hopes of developing a more empathetic appreciation for their struggles. Their upbringing. Their shortcomings. Their limitations and their silent cries for meaningful relief. None of us is perfect!

Having consideration for others means being respectful enough to lend a hand, especially when someone may be without a hand to give. Be generous and love the best way you know how, without being judgmental because you're unable to relate to the things that aren't so apparent. Not everything is about you. The sooner you understand that concept, the better off we all will be.

There is nothing foul about you. How long will it take before you realize that serving others is not a grudging task but actually the hallmark of an enriched character?

You can't live a perfect day without doing something for someone who will never be able to repay you.

–JOHN WOODEN

Having consideration for others may consist of going to the grocery store for your neighbors because they're unable to get there for themselves. Having consideration for others sometimes entails you doing a little bit more than they would do for you. This is what makes you so valuable.

You're at a store shopping and you decide to treat

yourself to something nice, but why not think about purchasing something for someone else too? It doesn't have to be expensive. How special would that make the other person feel? A genuine gesture of pure kindness. Obviously, you have a good heart. Nowadays, who considers the joy that can be brought to someone's heart when the person learns how much you really care about him/her? The relief you can contribute to a saddened heart upon the person learning that he/she was worthy of being remembered by you, for no apparent reason, is priceless. Think about how you might feel if someone unexpectedly gave you a gift for no other reason than because he/she appreciated you. Pretty special, huh? Life is about being selfless, not selfish!

It's quite simple—have enough respect and concern for people to help lighten their loads in thoughtful ways. No one is asking you to assume responsibility for the actions of others. We're candidly speaking about you becoming a decent individual with a glowing personality. Care for others as you would love for someone to care for you.

In having consideration for others, you must be careful not to become a burden. Sometimes we request things of people without being considerate for what they may have going on at the moment. You never want to become a weight; you should strive to be the person who removes them. Being inconsiderate causes damage to our souls. Who in their right mind wants to deal with a person who lacks the ability to be warmhearted and polite? Only an individual who is without tasteful manners.

If someone is kind enough to lend you something, make sure you are responsible enough to return it within a reasonable amount of time and, if possible, in better condition than when it was generously loaned to you. There is an old Zulu Proverb that says, "If you borrow an axe, return it with some of the ribs it has cut." If it's money that you have borrowed, there is no harm in adding a few extra dollars as a token of your appreciation.

 **JEWEL**

Do not pin yourself
in a position that
reveals eroded
manners. Always
have consideration
for other people. It is
a direct reflection of
what your character
is comprised of.

Humility Is Best

People with humility don't think
less of themselves; they just
think of themselves less.

—ANONYMOUS

YOU MAY BE the richest person in the world, with prestige befitting for a king or queen, and yet not even that should prevent you from being of service to others. Having the ability to overlook your personal status and extend your hand to help tend to the needs of those who are less fortunate indicates that you possess some level of humility.

It is a virtue that is constantly seeking to bring value and relief to someone else's life without consideration for what it may cost. Humility is forgetting about yourself while attempting to highlight the importance of people who are convinced that they have been forgotten. It is silently taking a back seat and basking in the joy of seeing others prosper.

It takes a large heart to do things that are voluminous in meaning, even in the moments when you may feel as though certain people aren't so deserving.

This is the essence of humility. We have no wish to judge the shortcomings of other people, only a need to help their pain go away. Develop an attitude of serving others, and your spiritual wealth will greatly increase. It is what you do in secret for other people that will permit your happiness and self-fulfillment to increase a thousand times over.

You won't always be able to immediately tell, but someone somewhere is desperately in need of your smile, your attentiveness, your hug, your love, your counsel, and your kind words. It's the smaller things that have proven to have the largest impact on other people's lives. You know, the kiss on the eye that's for no other reason than because the recipient is highly worthy. It'll come as a surprise to him/her and make the recipient ask the question, "Why me?" It's the unexpected show of generosity that will create a consciousness and realness that will plant a permanent smile on his/her face. A smile that brings the easing of a worried heart.

Inside humility can be found an even playing field that proves you are no better than the next person. Knowing humility enables us all to not only understand what it means to never act too big or too important to help those in need, but also reminds us to walk a silent walk that finds pleasure in giving praise to someone who is just as deserving, if not more.

The inability to be humble towards others is a direct reflection of the content of our hearts. It is impossible to know humility if you are preoccupied with yourself all of the time. Make it a priority to put others first sometimes, and that will infuse your relationships with a sparkling vitality. By doing so, you won't miss out on anything, but you will certainly gain everything that is worth something.

Humility must be a part of your lifestyle, not a random act you perform once, twice, or three times a year. Be an example of the humility that you would enjoy seeing in others. We lead only by example.

JEWEL

Humility is the glue that bonds us together. You for me and me for you.

—KENYATTA ANDINO

Accepting "No" for an Answer

Being able to accept "No" shouldn't
leave a bitter taste in your mouth.
It should highlight what level
of maturity you possess.

— DERRICK L. CRAWFORD

LIFE'S JOURNEY WILL bear you many disappointments. Things will not always swing in your favor; meaning, not every request or desire you seek to be filled by others will end with a delightful, "Yes." It shouldn't be a big deal. It's just the way it is.

When you ask someone to do something for you and the person refuses by telling you no or conveys to you that he/she is unable to help you at the moment, respect and accept that decision. There is no need to become angry because a person is unwilling or possibly unable to accommodate you when you feel the time is appropriate for you. It is a person's prerogative to tell you no without any explanation at all. What are you, five years old and still acting immature? Signs of maturity or a lack thereof become apparent when you demonstrate an inability to deal with rejection in a seasoned manner. This book is about learning to appreciate exquisite cuisines, not Gerber's baby food!

Becoming agitated or distraught after receiving a response that is not to your satisfaction should be disheartening. How could you become argumentative just because someone tells you no? There are a host of reasons why a person may not be able to assist you. Maybe you are being tested to see how well you accept refusals. Perhaps it's the wrong time, or it could be that the person is sincerely unable to help you. Sometimes, even if people want to assist you, they just can't, and so the only available option is to be honest and tell you no. Whatever the reason may be, never lose your composure. Hold your head up and accept no with the same amount of grace as if the answer were yes.

Hold up! Not so fast. There's a flip side to this lesson. You must also possess the courage to tell others no as well. Don't be so easy all the time. Having an understanding of when to refuse or deny someone is as equally as important as knowing how to accept no. There is a method for telling people no in a way that isn't agitatedly rude. If you feel as though you do not want to assist others, you owe it to yourself, as well as to them, to be completely honest. You should never feel ashamed to speak your mind respectfully. The last thing you want to do is mislead others into believing you are going to do something for them that you have no intention of doing. Acting in such a way leaves your character looking questionable.

We all have met our share of ingenuous people. You know, those who are practically dying for you to ask them for a favor just so they can tell you no when you need it most. Warning: it may hurt your feelings to realize that the person who denies you is the very same individual you've blessed on several occasions without the slightest hesitation. Don't think about it too much. Never sweat the small stuff, and whatever you do, don't ever speak of it. When you remind people of what they failed to do for you, it takes away from who you are. God blesses those who at least try to do for themselves.

> I am thankful for all those who said No to me. It's because of them I'm doing it myself.
>
> **—ALBERT EINSTEIN**

Yes, it's true. Sometimes through observation you may be able to tell that certain people you consider to be close to you are nothing more than envious of you. Not everyone will be able to complement the beauty of your character or respect the prosperity that seems to find your personality attractive. As a result, those people can be found secretly harboring ill feelings that cause them to impatiently wait for that one opportunity to deny you, no matter what the reason is.

If you truly want to show your compassion to those who deny you when you are really in need, forgive them. I promise you they will never forget the warmness of your heart. Why? Because it will literally serve as a reminder to them how petty they acted towards the one person who has never had anything less than respect for their character.

JEWEL

Accepting "no" should be done with grace.

—MAURICE PEARSON

Take a Peek at What it Is To Be Authentic

PEOPLE WHO DO authentic deeds from the goodness of their hearts are practically nonexistent anymore. What happened to the good ol' days when conversations were substantive and decent folks would lend a helping hand to the neighbors who found themselves in need?

Being authentic is nothing more than being real in what you say and what you do every single moment of your life! You don't have to come up with elaborate stories to entertain people in hopes of them accepting you. It's perfectly okay to admit that you have yet to experience life. Where is the harm in that?

Some people are early birds, while others are late bloomers. You will receive major cool points for being real, especially when in the company of those who've been around the block a few times. Let everything about you speak to your genuineness. Your actions. Your conversation, and even your walk. Let it all be exactly what God has provided you with. Wholeheartedly embrace who you are, without any exceptions.

Would you like to know something real? Your thoughts are a true reflection of your character and a testament to your current circumstances. Should your ideas and actions consist of untruths, your entire life will be without meaningful potential.

You don't have to lie to kick it. Just be yourself and all will be well. When was the last time you took a long, hard look at yourself in the mirror? You're already cool; there is no need to run around seeking validation from people. Fine tune what you have and press the go button. Being comfortable in who you are will show in your demeanor, and good people will naturally gravitate to you. Don't pretend to be anything other than who you are. What's so real about that? Doing anything other than being authentic prevents your character from someday obtaining greatness.

Like minds attract; just be cautious of attracting people who appear to be as genuine as you are, but who don't have your best interests at heart.

In your walk of life, you will encounter many people who will prove to be fickle, unreal, and extremely ungrateful for the things you and others do for them. Being the creative, successful force that you are will cause you to be swarmed by those who want to ingratiate themselves with you only because of your erupting potential. Oh, and sometimes due to the materialistic valuables you possess. When you fall out of favor, as we all do at some point in time, the love affair will suddenly come to a screeching halt. How will you know the likes of them? They are usually identified by being loud so that others can hear them proclaiming how much love they have for you or pretending like there's nothing in the world they wouldn't do for you. Nonsense. It's the talk of a drunkard! The humorous aspect of their charade will come to light whenever trouble is near and it's discovered it was them who personally vowed to stick by your side, no matter what. Once there is no longer an incentive for them, they will miraculously disappear. If you were truly in need, they wouldn't be anywhere to be found. This is how unauthentic people act.

Beware of those who come to you bearing smiles, pretending they have an abundance of compassion, knowing that their hearts are only filled with envy and deception. Their only objective is to deplete you of everything that has any type of value, including your creative inspiration. Allow your heart and soul to communicate their comfortability or lack thereof before you permit people to step beyond your comfort zone.

We all transmit vibrations. How else would you attempt to explain the uneasiness we feel when around certain people who are no good for us? All that's required is for you to be receptively attuned. Learn to pay attention to your inner voice. It is most vocal when you sit in complete silence.

Embrace everything that tells a pleasant tale of who you are. There shouldn't be a single witness to speak against your authenticity. Permit the smoothness of your personal music to guide you to a special place where you can comfortably allow the beat to ride out.

You're a winner! If you don't think so, then maybe you shouldn't be reading this book. No moral weakness exists in you for comparing your authenticity to the smoke and mirrors of others, particularly when you have encountered more than your share of deceitful relationships where people masquerade as being real, but their allegiance secretively goes to those who are untrustworthy and dangerously cunning.

Periodically, evaluate yourself to be certain that your actions are sincere. If you cannot be authentic within, how is it possible to be authentic with someone else? Once you're able to create a strong foundation that consist of morals and sweet values, be willing to die before you violate them in any fashion. Should your true nature be that of a snake, vulture, rat, or cleverly disguised wolf, it's only a matter of time before you will be discovered.

 **JEWEL**

Even the cover of night has an allotted moment before it is exposed to the light of day.

Faith Is More Than Saying You Believe

> If you have no confidence in self
> you are twice defeated in the race
> of life. With confidence you have
> won even before you have started.
>
> **—HON. MARCUS MOSIAH GARVEY**

EVERY PERSON HAS fantasized, in some capacity, about what shall become of his/her life. Losing hope does not mean that your dream is deferred; although, sometimes it may become blemished when the means to attainment no longer seems to avail itself to our personal cause. In particular, after striving so hard to make things happen. Don't worry yourself over spoiled milk. Starting today, begin to have faith and true belief in the things you want for yourself. Visualize them and be confident that you will receive them.

Try going to a quiet place and sitting comfortably while focusing on what it is that you desire. Step by step, imagine playing your part to the fullest. Maybe you want a new profession, a larger bank account, or a better relationship with someone who is very important to you. Look over every step that you must take in order to succeed.

Take note of how you speak to people, how you dress, and the message your body language conveys. Speak with confidence in yourself. Dress as if you're someone respectable and walk with your head held up high. Visualize it all. Do not leave anything out. Continue rehearsing that beautiful vision and speak what you want into existence. "I will become better at _____." Fill in the blank with your own personal affirmations. Don't just speak it into existence. You must think it into existence as well. If you lack faith in what you are trying to obtain, it will never manifest itself.

Do not stop repeating to yourself the steps you need to take in order to arrive at your destination. Convincingly tell yourself that you know the way and that you refuse to allow anyone to hinder you from getting there. Only you can prevent your success from occurring. You are in full control.

Each day, walk your walk. Forget about what other people may be thinking or whispering behind your back. Perform as if you have already met success. Tell yourself you will be successful no matter what you choose to do in life. Go back to the mirror you're always looking in and tell yourself out loud what changes you wish to make today. Believe in your abilities. It is very important.

Now you are beginning to get a taste of what successful people go through in order to program their minds to become achievers. They practically "will" themselves into success by constantly entertaining positive thoughts, day in and day out. The exact same thing happens all over again the next day. It is a continuous process that never fails to provide tangible results.

You're aiming for something exceptional. When obstacles appear in your path, climb over them or go around them, just be sure to remain steadfast. Keep talking it out. Whatever it is you want, make sure you work hard towards that end. Most people don't have the slightest clue that such an intangible force exists, let alone recognize how powerful it is. Don't play with it. At least, twenty minutes each day should be dedicated to this *very important cause*!

This is the power of faith: belief that anything you put your mind to is possible. Change your thoughts, and your circumstances will faithfully follow. It is obligatory for you to believe that you can do it.

 **JEWEL**

Now faith is the substance of things hoped for, the evidence of things not seen.

– HEBREWS 11:1

Jealous for What Reason?

The wildwood birds ... sang in
concert, without pride, without
envy, without jealousy ...

—SIMON POKAGON

WAIT A MINUTE! They must be speaking of someone other than you, right? You are jealous of who and for what reason? Let's explore this nasty, selfish emotion.

We have been down this road before. When you harbor such weak thoughts, eventually you will begin to develop negative mental habits that transform into a mental sickness and a hardened heart.

Suspicion, anger, worry, distrust, and jealousy are all negative emotions that if not banned from your mind, will literally drive you insane. You know how to get rid of such thoughts. What seems to be the hold up?

What could possibly be the reason you are jealous of someone else? Certainly you possess enough knowledge to help you obtain whatever it is you put your mind to. There are a lot of people who are without a fraction of the guidance you now find yourself receiving. All you have to do is develop and cultivate your talents. You can have anything you desire, if only you would learn to whole-heartedly apply yourself. If anything, people should be jealous of you.

Jealousy is a trait that's possessed by those who are mentally weak and secretly envious of you. Such people have no mental discipline, nor the ability to formulate a plan for obtaining what they want from life. There is nothing weak about you and definitely no reason for you to be jealous of anyone else. Once again, what could anyone possibly have that you cannot put yourself in a position to acquire? Nothing at all. Pull yourself together and stop allowing your emotions to get the best of you.

Being jealous conveys that you have a heap of inse-curities. It paints you as a person who is more inclined to be an instrument utilized for dividing people, as opposed to one who unites them. You make no time for getting to know a person for who they are; instead, you're comfortably consumed with emotions that are literally eating you alive. Are you jealous because someone is favored more than you, because he/she does things a little more flavorful than you, or because he/she holds a position you feel should have been yours? These are all erroneous reasons to be jealous.

You cannot expect to show others the flaws in their ways if you are busy harboring your own ill feelings that have absolutely no validation.

 **JEWEL**

If two elephants have a quarrel in the forest, the trees and leaves there are in trouble.

—AKAN PROVERB

Being a Liar Won't Get You Far

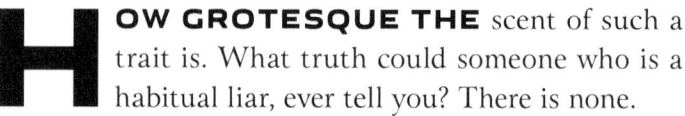

To tell a falsehood is like the cut
of a saber, for though the wound
may heal the scar will remain.

—PERSIAN PROVERB

HOW GROTESQUE THE scent of such a trait is. What truth could someone who is a habitual liar, ever tell you? There is none.

The liar's candle lasts till evening.

—TURKISH PROVERB

People who feel an overwhelming need to bend and twist the truth to fit their perceptions usually suffer from some type of psychosis. They are constantly in denial of having said anything that is factually inaccurate. You will come to learn that liars have an overestimation of their self-worth; meaning, their lifestyles will always intentionally be amplified in comparison to yours. It's a tactic utilized to diminish your self-esteem and belittle your wonderful accomplishments.

A liar has no chance for gaining moral richness, and under no circumstances are you to have faith in anything he/she says. It doesn't matter how big or small the lie is. All lies fall under the same umbrella. Once someone proves to be a liar, it's best for you to keep your distance, or you run the risk of having to second-guess everything coming from that person's lips. There is no consideration for whose feelings may be hurt.

The person who feels a need to lie all the time has no decency. Liars could care less about having scruples about how others may perceive them once the truth has been discovered. If you provide them with a single opportunity, they will try to spin a new lie in an attempt to cover up the initial falsehood. It is of little importance whether you are family, a stranger, or someone who cares from a place deep within. No one is exempt. If someone lies to you once, it's only a matter of time before he/she lies to you again.

....

One seldom meets a lonely lie.

—AMERICAN PROVERB

....

There is an old saying: "Fool me once, shame on you. Fool me twice, shame on me." While there are a few folks who may be deserving of a second chance, you need to be cautious about whom you give a second chance. And do not make the mistake of providing people with a third chance to do you wrong. Yes, sometimes it can be a bit difficult to heed, especially when the person is family or an individual we have loved for an extended period of time. At least try to remain conscious of the fact that you cannot place much faith in what the person says, regardless of whether he/she was trying to harm you or claimed to have been protecting you.

Be cautious of what spews from the mouths of liars. They have repeated their lies so many times what they say has actually become a truth in their own minds.

....

Truthful lips endure forever, but a
lying tongue lasts only a moment.

–PROVERBS 12:19

....

Liars enjoy having others believe they are more slithery than a snake and can fool the world at whim. Through their pathological illness, they have convinced themselves they are able to outwit everyone. They exist only on a base of lies, and they will say whatever they must in order to get what they want from you. The truth is never thought of as being a plausible option because they are terrified that so many other things they were untruthful about will come to light.

People who find delight in mingling with liars do so because, in one way or another, they are like-minded. How are you able to practice having morals and exercise good judgement yet continue to find comfort in those whose habits have been proven to be immoral? Don't you understand that when you compromise what you stand for, your value as a decent human being depreciates?

Liars are the true culprits of social danger. Do not destroy your integrity because you have failed to be indiscriminate with those who are truly unworthy of your companionship. Try to remember, much can be discerned from the company we choose to keep.

It is better to tell the truth than to be branded as a liar for the rest of your life.

....
If you sow falsehood you reap deceit.

—AFRICAN PROVERB
....

How honorable do you think your character would be if you were known for having a forked tongue?

 JEWEL

Stay true to the words that you speak and you will never have to worry about the order in which they were spoken.

The Depths of Loyalty

If you owe allegiance to more
than one person you are lost.

—AKAN PROVERB

LOYALTY IS MUCH more than an eye-catching tattoo. It is a virtue worthy of a lifelong commitment, without the pain of provisions.

Any relationship rich in substance deserves to be complemented with devotion. Meaning, occupying selfish thoughts of only yourself will never find admirable support because true loyalty is mutual. If you do not agree, then someone is being setup for a serious let down. The intoxicating scent of loyalty is one that must be appropriately cherished forever.

Loyalty entails sacrificing—your time. Your inclination to speak when solely charged with the duty to listen without being argumentative. Your last, and occasionally your portion, especially if it helps to place someone else in a better position. It is weathering struggles together, no matter how burdensome things may be. The pleasure of knowing a person is loyal enough to endure uncertainties with you is sufficient to bring comfort to any heart found wallowing in distress.

Loyalty is a continuous sharing of truth, despite your uncomfortableness at the thought of being admonished for failing to do better. At least someone cares enough to enlighten you. When a person understands loyalty, he/she doesn't have to be told, "There's only one side to be on." There is no straddling the fence or testing the water to see if something more rewarding can be gained from playing on the other side.

Loyalty is for times of betterment and unpleasantness. It is supposed to be sustained through wealth or impoverishment. Captivity or independence. It shouldn't matter whether the person you are committed to is suffering from a disorder or has a clean bill of health.

> Loyalty isn't everything in such
> a fine exchange of harmonious
> mutuality. It is the only thing.
> **—LA'SHANDA C. CRAWFORD**

Because many of us know the story of pain that is frequently associated with having been betrayed and can identify with the discomforts of being emotionally scarred, we must be cautious of who we choose to extend our loyalties to. Understand with certainty who your true companions are. You'll know for sure when the time is right, but for now, you only need to know that the average person who you think has some type of concern for your well-being will never be able to consistently demonstrate a pattern of faithfulness. Does this critique appear to be a bit harsh? Perhaps. But the ability to observe wisely and listen intently will provide justice for the truth of the matter.

Happiness can be found in the composition of loyalty. Should you ever encounter such a jewel, it would be wise to protect your emotional vulnerabilities until others can prove to you who they really are. Those who are truly loyal may be as rare as ancient Egyptian cloth.

Family and friends are usually the ones who we are most loyal to. Whether or not they manifest their loyalties to us is a question that sometimes remains ambiguous. If you are one who proudly wears your allegiance on your sleeve and feel as though the depth of loyalty from others isn't the same, you must make the necessary adjustments to prevent having regrets later.

Loyalty involves tales of courage, nursed passions, and love without limitations. Anyone who is truly loyal to you deserves nothing less than your devotion until the end of time. No matter what people who care about you may be going through, stick close to them. Protect them mentally and emotionally, as well as physically. Encourage them to reach higher, and never lose your touch of how easy it is for you to show them you have always had their backs. It will evoke a priceless smile. Provide them with an opportunity to experience the rapture of your dedication, even when it may be a bit challenging for you to gather the strength to give it your all.

Learning to endure their pain and hardships with a showing of loyalty should come with ease. There are very few things more heartwarming than discovering it was the person who has always proclaimed to love and never betray you who has defended your honor, even when you were not available to defend it yourself.

Loyalty can be spotted in the eyes of the person who continues to be by your side well after the storm has past. The sun will shine again, and that is when you will be able to look towards it with a gracious smile and a feeling of blessedness for being provided with someone who is tailor-made just for you.

Never dishonor the gift of loyalty. It is precious, yet becoming more and more uncommon. It is sacred to those who are sincere. It is a cherished virtue in the hearts of those who would prefer dying by it before ever entertaining the thought of betraying it.

J E W E L

When two people understand the depth of loyalty, they won't have to waste time trying to express the emotions of their soul.

— MERCEDES CARTER

Being Anxious Causes Many Mistakes

Being anxious prevents our mind
from knowing the tranquility of
a refreshingly calm, silence.

—CARL CHESTER

THERE IS NOTHING more detrimental to your plans than being anxious. You are not a kid who's anxiously waiting for the arrival of Christmas day. Maturity of the mind demands that you be in full control of your emotions and cognizant of the fact that being too eager is a sign of someone who is without self-discipline. Relax. Take your time and try not to be so temperamental.

Have you ever noticed how certain birds impatiently swarm and fight over crumbs of bread that are thrown to them? No calming of thoughts before making decisions and no inclination to embrace a clear perspective before attempting to appropriately manage emotions. This is the mentality of folks who live life anxiously.

Calming of the mind: observe closely and you'll

notice there is always at least one cautious bird sitting patiently waiting for their moment to peacefully enjoy a crumb or two. The anxiety of one bird naturally causes anxiety in others, but for the bird who knows discipline, a rewarding choice shall always be allocated.

Thoroughly contemplate the things you have to do before you do them. A calming of the mind will bring you the correct answer if you do not act anxiously.

Having an unsettled mind can cause us to overlook important details. When you possess the ability to be mentally disciplined, it will help you relax and effectively maintain your composure while under pressure. Are you acting out of being anxious or are you actually methodically thinking your way through troubling situations?

Take note of how dignitaries of foreign countries conduct themselves. The women handle themselves with a tremendous amount of poise and the gentleman display prestige. Very seldom will you witness professionals acting outside of their character. Be patient and allow things to come to you.

When you leave home each morning, the world will be waiting to see how you perform. How you treat others when things aren't particularly going your way. What you produce from what little you have.

Prove that you are certain of yourself and confident about the road you must travel in order to get to where you need to be. Conduct yourself with a touch of class!

JEWEL

Being anxious can
cause us to miss
crucial directions.
Not everyone has the
luxury of wasting gas.

A Taste of Ambition

The smaller the lizard, the greater
its hope of becoming a crocodile.

—AFRICAN PROVERB

AMBITION CAN BE considered the workhorse of desire. It is a feeling of urge and hunger that propels you to complete your goals, regardless of how difficult the process may seem to be. It is inspiration that fuels your *will* to perform on a level that's your absolute best. It is an eagerness to arise early in the morning and put your best foot forward until, at last, you have managed to succeed.

Some people possess more ambition than others. Many don't have the slightest clue as to what it is or how powerful it can be. Individuals with strong minds and a burning determination to accomplish things have cultivated and developed this remarkable quality. Success is not possible without having an ambitious disposition.

How is it nurtured? It's nurtured by completing every task you embark upon. Do not become deterred from doing what you need to do in order to meet triumph. Stay focused no matter how challenging the obstacles in your path may become. The reward goes to the man or woman who eagerly devises a plan to navigate around obstacles and continue to meet his or her initial objectives.

Utilize the forces against you to your advantage. Make it your business to learn of the secretive power that lies in being able to transform negative situations into positive, beneficial works of art. While in the process, smile, knowing that it's the energy of those who wish to see you fail that is being used for additional motivation towards your success.

Let every attempt you make in life be nothing short of your absolute best. Each day tell yourself aloud, "I will do better today than I did yesterday!" Don't just say it once or twice; repeat it often throughout the day. Say it as if you really mean it. Your DNA is coded with greatness. Understand that it is in your best interest to become hopeful and excited for what may be, especially when attainment is in reach.

There is no need to hide your ambition. Modesty has an appropriate place. Now is your time to step up and lead the way. Others see in us what we sometimes fail to see in ourselves; as a result, we'll be expected to perform on a level that surpasses those who are nothing more than average.

You should be extremely proud of this newly acquired lesson, for it shall never allow you to be without a gust of wind to your back.

Now that ambition has been introduced to you, it finds itself curious as to how you shall apply it. Go ahead, don't be shy. Show everyone how vigorous you will be in maintaining the integrity of such a precious jewel.

 **JEWEL**

Let not the familiarity
of being ambitious
escape your
acquaintance, lest
failure be the fate of all
your attempts in life.

Common Sense Is a Rarity

....

Though you would like to beat
the dog, you must consider
the master's face as well.

– BURMESE PROVERB

....

IF YOU THINK about it, common sense amongst the masses appears to be not so common anymore. We haven't forgotten how to do basic arithmetic, so how have we failed to exercise our ability to make basic, intelligent decisions?

Common sense should propel you to think before you do things. Is what you are doing the right thing to do? Is the course you're taking appropriate? When we think before we say things or take certain actions, it becomes probable that the outcome will be more respectable.

Common sense demands we utilize discretion in all of our endeavors. Allow your wisdom to flow through all of your actions, speech, and relations with others. Maintain a levelheadedness about yourself.

Using common sense with a willingness to pay

attention to detail and to others who may be affected by our actions will help us become better individuals. All it takes is for us to think and act accordingly. We are natural logicians without the principles and laws to complicate everything.

Prove you have common sense by demonstrating the soundness of your practical decisions.

> No one tests the depth of
> a river with both feet.
> **—ASHANTI PROVERB**

JEWEL

Just because a person has some form of intelligence doesn't necessarily mean they possess common sense.

—VAUGHN WRIGHT

Having Compassion Will Win You the Hearts of Many

....

Our human compassion
combines us, one to another.

—NELSON MANDELA

....

WHAT WOULD THE contents of our souls look like if we were never presented with an opportunity to exercise our compassion? For some, they may never know, but for others, providing time to help those in need is a way of life. It is our calling. Look to the generous and unassuming acts of Mother Teresa. When you look up the word "generous" in a good dictionary, you should find a picture of her affixed for all the world to see. Compassion is a gift of mercy.

People, animals, and insects don't necessarily have to find themselves in an unfortunate situation to be helped by you; all that is required is for you to feel an urge to be of assistance. Listen to your heart. It will never lead you astray. Those who know what it is to be compassionate do a very good job anticipating the suffering and pain of others.

Not every person you meet will know the tenderness of a compassionate heart. In fact, be mindful of the individual who selectively dispenses acts of compassion. This person will smile in your face and pretend to have a huge heart, but someplace within he/she finds discomfort with who he/she is. True acts of compassion come from the soul, not from afterthoughts.

The compassionate tendencies you have towards others should never be spoken of. Pay no attention to those who visually witness your acts of kindness. All that should concern you is the fact you took action because of what you felt in your heart. There are no accolades or rewards given for decency. Use discretion and be modest about your deeds.

Please don't ever find amusement in someone else's suffering. Be the person who provides nutritious food for those who are mentally and physically hungry, and think not twice before offering clothing and a safe shelter to those who find themselves without much. Give leniency and sound advice to those who commit wrongs. For there is always a chance their souls may, too, be salvageable.

Show compassion to those who are able to recognize they have made a mistake and sincerely wish they would have acted or spoken differently. Only if a person's regret for their wrongdoing is sincere should you accept his/her apology and show the compassion of your heart. Refrain from trusting any person who is quick to dispense punishment. It is a gift, not a commandment from God!

In your daily pursuit for truth, you will encounter people who create displeasure in your heart. Oh how repugnant the scent of a wicked soul is. Show compassion and do your very best to alleviate the pain others have caused. In an attempt to preserve the goodness of your heart and prevent the beauty of your generosity from being tainted, it's important for you to learn how to forgive the iniquity of those who are ignorant.

For all who are truly gracious and strive hard to live life righteously, know that compassion is a part of your true identity. Be certain you are never taken for a fool because you chose to give compassion to those who smiled in your face, knowing wholeheartedly they will never have anything more than contempt in their hearts. It is virtually impossible to have compassion for others if you have never known compassion for yourself.

....

The delicate and infirm go for sympathy, not to the well and buoyant, but to those who have suffered like themselves.

—CATHERINE ESTHER BEECHER

....

146

JEWEL

The world has a
shortage of people
who are compassionate
enough to take
action in the wake
of silent cries from
those who are truly
in need of help.

—MERCEDES CARTER

The Beauty of Education

Education is the work of your entire life.

—HAITIAN PROVERB

EDUCATION IS WHAT helps us to advance in life. Without affording yourself an opportunity to gain general or specialized knowledge, you cannot expect to excel beyond those who are ordinary.

There is absolutely nothing comical about lacking the capability to read or comprehend, or failing to know the basic mechanics of arithmetic. We're not even discussing geometry, calculus, or mind-boggling trigonometry. It's mind-boggling in the sense that it would be tortuous to those who feel as though they are unable to understand the purpose for acquiring such necessary math skills.

Is it okay to live a trifling life, one that forces you to depend on others to satisfy your needs? I think not, but indeed, this is exactly what your life will consist of if you don't know the pleasure of some sort of education.

Educate yourself and witness opportunities spring

up before your very eyes. We are all capable of knowing some form of intelligence. With only 5 percent of our brain being utilized on a daily basis, what untapped potential lies dormant in the remaining 95 percent? Our brains are always churning, waiting for a chance to be put to work. When we provide them with nothing that is challenging or constructive, they accept whatever rubbish we provide. Think about all of the useless information we feed our minds each day and then honestly tell the world you haven't the slightest clue as to why you are destitute.

Education will bring about solid ideas that can be utilized for tomorrow's challenges. You owe it to yourself to obtain a decent education. Give your thoughts a chance to aspire to heights that are unfamiliar. Become excited about the unlimited potential that awaits awakening.

Vocabulary. Get in the habit of looking up words you don't know the meanings of. It not only helps to develop your comprehension skills, but it will also enhance your communication skills. Challenge your mind. Strive to learn at least three new words every day. Don't just memorize them. Utilize them or you'll lose your touch.

Find out what your hidden talents are and cultivate them. Ask plenty of questions that will help arouse your curiosity. You cannot allow boredom to find a safe haven in your mind.

Learn the valuable lessons of those who came before you. Thoroughly research their biographies. Familiarize yourself with history, science, sociology, psychology, and the mechanics of writing.

Read! Read! Read! You should try to read for at

least two hours a day. Study what you have read; don't just skim through it.

While we're discussing education, try to remember this: do not become accustomed to being in the company of people who are less intelligent than you are. Sure, it's perfectly okay to share your knowledge, but you must not form a habit of continually trying to school or educate those who insist on being nothing more than ignorant and who haven't the slightest concern for your vision.

Too much of anything is not good for us. A moment where you unconsciously allow the ignorance of others' bad habits to seep into your subconscious mind should never arise. The price you had to pay to acquire your knowledge is entirely too expensive for it to be dispensed amongst those who have no vision for their future.

Education can be likened to a game of chess. If you engage people who are unable to properly challenge your skills, you will never advance. Be determined to learn from those who are more intelligent than you. In doing so, you will find continuous growth with a curiosity for what is next to come. Study the ways of those who are cultured and interestingly quiet in their walks of life.

Would you like to know something else? If you build a well-balanced academic education and truly understand the things you speak of, people will eagerly want to listen to you, especially if they are unfamiliar with that which you are speaking about. If possible, provide those who are trying to help themselves with a hand that will help pull them up from their plights.

Be careful not to overextend yourself and risk tumbling back into unpleasant circumstances.

Cherish your education. It will begin by utilizing what you have to its fullest.

JEWEL

Education has no end.

—SWAHILI PROVERB

There Is Nothing Attractive About Being Needy

Even a loyal companion will quickly grow weary of the hand that is always extended with so many expectations of being catered to.

—CHRISTOPHER MURRAY

A **PERSON OF YOUR** quality has no business whatsoever being needy. No excuse exists that can explain how you are mentally and spiritually wealthy yet continue to find a need to beg others for the things you are perfectly capable of obtaining by the powers invested in you.

If only you would at least try. Put forth the effort and have complete faith in yourself. I don't get it. What's the draw? Surely you cannot possibly find comfort in leeching off others, or can you? Have you ever considered the disgust of onlookers? All they can visualize are images of you in a mentally broken state, one that embodies weakness, disloyalty, and the weighing of the caliber of soul that has been wasted.

Being able to provide for yourself can persuade people to have a positive opinion of you and view you as someone who has integrity. When we act as though we're constantly in need of things that are inconsequential, it ruins our reputation and causes our status to drop tremendously.

Asking others for things you are perfectly capable of getting makes you appear as though you lack knowledge, heart, and pizzazz. How can you consider yourself a provider if you are always in someone's face asking for this or asking for that? Have you no shame? No sense of embarrassment due to your refusal to do what you need to do for yourself? Get out and get some.

Never provide those who secretly despise you with the pleasure of knowing a single moment when you had to ask them or were overheard asking someone else for anything that will paint you as a person whose nasty habits consist of depending on others.

Being self-sufficient, for some odd reason, provokes those who are repugnant and unfailingly in search of flaws in your character. A display of strength through confidence seems to upset them. This is the prime reason why it is important to socialize with those who are more refined. Those who have achieved or are busy trying to have no wish to gloat or worry about highlighting your shortcomings. Mingle with those who possess style and grace, and you shall learn how to fish for yourself.

Chronologically establish your priorities and you will never have to ask for the things you enjoy.

Responsible people ration their portions in a way that prevents them from knowing what it is to be needy.

Showing a tendency for being needy is for those who are unable to make things happen. Should there come a time when you are truly in need of something that someone else has, be certain to exchange something of equal or greater value. Don't get caught up with arguing over the difference in value between what you have to offer and what a person has that you want. Leave the petty haggling to those who cherish the color of their pennies.

 **JEWEL**

Continually begging for additional resources sooner or later handicaps the mind's ability to become creatively self-sufficient.

—DAJA WILLIAMS

Being Courageous
Is Honorable

> I learned that courage was not the
> absence of fear, but the triumph over it.
> The brave man is not he who does not
> feel afraid, but he who conquers fear.
>
> **—NELSON R. MANDELA**

LET'S BE HONEST with ourselves. No one respects a coward, but we love to rally around the man or woman who demonstrates what courage looks like while in the face of some type of adversity.

Having guts is more than a showing of physical bravery or the pursuit of strength while in the midst of danger. Courage is having an ability to bypass the fear that usually hinders us from moving forward in a productive way. To be courageous is to be wise in matters that are challenging.

> Courage is the fruit of a
> decision made in the heart.
>
> **—AFRICAN PROVERB**

Being courageous is more than standing up for yourself. It entails standing up for those who are being taken advantage of. Not everyone will have what it takes to stand up and defend themselves against those who love to oppress. No, you cannot save the world, but it is definitely possible for you to do a little more than your allotted share, and that is what makes you strong.

In difficult times, standing up and voicing what you believe is an excellent example of being courageous. If you feel something isn't right, stand up and speak on it. The worst thing a person can ever do is see an injustice being committed and choose to say nothing at all. In what way are you any different than the person who is committing an indecent act against humanity? Don't just speak about it. If you are in the right, shout about it. Scream and holler until they hear you loud and clear!

Arguably, one of the most daring explorations of your life will consist of understanding the truth about who you are and learning how best to develop a mental discipline that can help you transform your thoughts and your behavior.

....

The hardest thing for people
to see is themselves.

—SHIH CHENG YEN

....

Be honest with yourself. It takes great courage to critique your shortcomings. You cannot highlight the good in you without possessing the nerve to underline all that is incomplete. All corrections begin with a sincere reflection in the mirror.

....

As a rock on the sea shore, stand firm,
and let not the dashing of the waves
disturb you. Raise your head like a
tower on the hill, and the arrows of
fortune drop at your feet. In the instant
danger, the courage of your heart
will sustain you; and the steadiness
of your mind beareth you through.

– KEMETIC PROVERB

....

JEWEL

Whatever a courageous man desires to do, he does.

– AKAN PROVERB

Nosy People Are Hard to Trust

Those who feel an overwhelming desire to meddle in other's affairs, must be scrutinized with caution.

—TRINA HILL

WHY IS IT you continue to be so interested in other's affairs? Weren't you taught that being a news box is very offensive? As if you didn't already know. It creates a distaste for your presence and serves as proof that you are incapable of finding something constructive to do with your free time.

Your lifestyle isn't supposed to emulate a daytime soap opera. You know, those daytime drama series that are comprised of meddling and constant prying into business that in no way pertains to those who pry. I mean, if you see it differently, try enlightening us as to what benefits can be received from being intrusive. If you consider yourself to be a part of the real world, you should already know there is absolutely no reason for you to be concerned with anything that is the least of your business.

Maybe you enjoy people being suspicious of you. Perhaps you find it pleasurable having no life and being miserable, bitter, and untrustworthy. See, the peculiar thing about being nosy is that once you've been pegged with having such a nasty habit, it becomes virtually impossible to turn back the hands of time. Who will trust you? Who could find comfort in a person who asks entirely too many personal questions, questions that are without substantive thought and totally irrelevant? When you're dealing with folks who do not have much on their minds, they tend to ask thoughtless questions: small talk, in hopes of getting you to reveal sensitive information. Don't trust it!

Restrain your impulse to be meddlesome. Should you ever witness people running up the street to investigate a situation that has absolutely nothing to do with them, resist the urge to be curious. What satisfaction do you gain from immediately dropping what you are doing just to fulfill your urge to be nosy? Whatever is going on up the street, it has nothing to do with you. It doesn't concern you, nor does it make any sense for you to be there and in the way.

Check it out. No person of substance is fond of the individual who snoops around and invades others' privacy. It's bad enough that with every step we take someone in an undisclosed location is scrutinizing our moves, but for you to intentionally trample on the private shelters of others is unforgivable. Overstepping our limits can cause problems, not only for ourselves, but for those whom we have relations with on a daily basis.

Excuse me? Did you ask, "What are the characteristics of a nosy person?" Well, classmates, through observation, listening, and personally having several calloused experiences, I can tell you that such people are foolhardily loquacious. They are without sensibility.

Boundaries entwined with integrity and morals will never discover a home in the hearts of those who are disgracefully unpleasant. Please inform us how you can confidently consider leaning on someone who has proven, on numerous occasions, to be without the mental discipline needed to restrain his/her impulses? You cannot. And so your only option is nothing more than to consciously infuse your life with the wise.

If you give serious thought to what has been said, you have to agree. No matter who you are or what position you occupy in life, you have no right to inject yourself into others' affairs. One day you may hear or see something that has nothing to do with you. Keep doing whatever it is you were doing. The world is dramatic enough without having to consider your faulty observations, stretched truths, and hidden motives. Sit back and focus on what you have going on.

Has someone specifically addressed you? No? Then why are you so closely paying attention and listening to everything that has absolutely nothing to do with you? It is easy to envision a world where everyone is respectful and well behaved, but when you learn to have true understanding, you will realize that entertaining such thoughts of a perfect world amounts to nothing more than a figment of your wildest imagination. Keep it practical, and let your journey be a well-respected one.

Now that you know a little more, do not act as if you haven't been informed of the stench of being nosy.

JEWEL

Never, under any circumstances, trust anyone who cannot mind their own business.

A Method for Changing Your Bad Habits

....

Habit, if not resisted, soon
becomes necessity.

—ST. AUGUSTINE

....

THE CRIPPLING HABITS that have ensnared our potential for growth have occurred only after we have continued to duplicate specific thoughts, behaviors, and actions. Our thoughts, having gone uncorrected for so long, eventually mutate into a habit that feels perfectly natural.

Each time we do something that is as common as putting our socks on, we are firmly embedding that particular practice in our minds. The next time you put your socks on, try to be conscious of which sock you placed on your foot first or which shoe you are in the habit of putting on first. You've never paid much attention to it because it is a perfectly normal, comfortable habit.

A constant use of obscene language while attempting to articulate yourself becomes habitual, thus preventing you from respectfully expressing your thoughts with intellectual precision. Ruminating day to day about things that hold the possibility of crippling your mental growth leads you directly to a pool of unpleasant habits.

The anatomy of our brain can be likened to putty. Due to the softness of putty, the slightest pressure applied enables it to be easily manipulated to form a configuration of our imagination. With each thought we occupy and every action that is executed, an impression is literally forged in our brains. The deeper the impression is, the more likely we are to continue to do the same things, utilizing the same methods; our thoughts are inclusive. This is why we are so predictable.

A consistency in the patterns of our thoughts, actions, and behaviors causes us to become self-complacent; as a result, immediate preference is given to familiar thoughts and actions. No wonder it feels so uncomfortable to learn new ways of doing things. This is the crippling effect of our bad habits.

Once an impression is forged upon our brains, it will never vanish. Yes, it is possible to change our thoughts and behaviors, but the old impression, which is more than likely crammed with our bad habits, will remain intact indefinitely.

Try envisioning the Mississippi River, or any river you may be familiar with. After millennia of guiding turbulent water, the constant pressure causes a riverbed to form. Think about how nearly impossible it would be to form a new channel and completely do away with the old. Our thoughts and actions have the same effect upon our cerebrums.

Unlike the New Year's resolutions we make, we

cannot vow to create new habits in place of our old habits and then fall short of being vigilantly devoted to the new habits. When a negative impulse arises, quickly dismiss and replace it with a positive action or thought. Basically, all you are doing is substituting a negative impulse with the positive reinforcement of a good habit. The negative impulses that we are used to harboring (the negative self-talk that attempts to convince us to do all the wrong things) will appear like an agitated craving. For example, say you have a bad habit of unconsciously throwing your garbage anyplace, aside from where it's supposed to be disposed of. Now that you have moral intelligence and actually pay closer attention to what you're thinking and what you are doing, your conscious awareness persuades you to hold on to the trash until you can find a trash bin. Normally, you wouldn't have blinked an eye before making the decision to act impulsively.

We rid ourselves of negative impulses by being conscious of the voices in our heads that try to get us to say and do the right things. It is a choice between right and wrong, and this is one of the beauties of having moral intelligence. Each time we substitute a good thought in place of a negative impulse, we create a stronger impression (through repetition), and before we know it, new and improved channels that hold a host of positive habits form in our brains. One that instinctively focuses on doing the right thing, opposed to choosing the unconscionable things we do when we believe no one is looking.

Give those new thoughts a lot of warm attention. Be proud of yourself for being able to make a change.

Caution: you must stay away from everything that has the potential to cause you to relapse and resort to your old way of thinking and acting.

Surround yourself with decent people who do not feel a need to use offensive language when expressing themselves. Turn the rap music down a few notches. It's not a luxury you can afford at this juncture of development. Try a touch of jazz or Wolfgang Amadeus Mozart, music that will permit you to hear yourself think clearly. Read books that offer food for thought. These are the secrets behind providing your brain with strong, positive messages.

Never make an exception or let down your guard. Stay strong! If you accommodate a negative impulse today, you will undoubtedly grant another reprieve for the same bad habit next week, and all that you have worked so hard to obtain will be lost forever. Continue to persevere. Anything worth having takes time to firmly establish. This is why those who are recovering addicts take the rehabilitation of their addictions one day at a time.

Until you have made a conscious decision to change your ways, nothing you have read will be of any help to you. In fact, you have wasted your time if you do not feel an urge to change your habits and become a better person. Not for others, but for yourself. You certainly have the knowledge; use it to your advantage. Cultivate morality and do not be afraid to embrace virtues.

Move forward cautiously and worry not about the unpleasant past you have turned your back on.

 **JEWEL**

Don't ever be afraid to change your bad habits, unless you don't mind being at the bottom.

–JANEE JOHNSON

Morals Are Wonderful Boundaries

WITHOUT A SINCERE wish to acknowledge and cultivate the virtues that are naturally sheltered under our moral intelligence, we shall never experience anything outside of the conditions of poverty, disease of the heart, or a morbid mind.

If we feel a sincere need to have a bit of faith in our moral structure and maintain strict control over our misguided impulses, we will come to know what it is to have morals of great value.

The brilliancy of our minds is worthy of awe. But it is our ill-fated steps, excessive chatter, and transgressions against what we claim to stand for that provoke others to be mistrustful and look at us with contempt.

No one should ever have the privilege of persuading you to believe that his/her standard of morals makes your standard less meaningful. Make no mistake about it. Your truth is always going to equate to another person's dishonesty. Meaning, what you believe in your heart to be correct, another person may swear on his/her life to know differently. No big deal! To you be your story and to them be theirs, just as long as yours is one that rings supreme.

Tainted water (crime) has enticed us to drink it while we're in our moments of disillusionment and thirst. Having seen the ill effects and tremendous loss it has caused us to suffer, we have vowed to never drink it again. Only through the vigilant eyes of our morals and promise to exercise righteous conduct will our inclination for doing wrong and thinking negatively have a chance to bypass the land of outcast.

There is no question about it. With strength and the guidance of our morals, we shall rise out of our weakened conditions and arrive in a realm that will permit us to meet our needs, as well as those of humanity.

Without possessing the jewels of morals—well, you should never be curious enough to learn about such an unstable ending.

 **JEWEL**

Live by your morals.

The Discomforts of Poverty

....
Empty sacks will never stand upright.

—ENGLISH PROVERB
....

POVERTY STRICKEN. HAVE you yet to grow tired of your present conditions? How long will it take before you arrive at the conclusion that you, and only you, are solely responsible for exiting the state of being poor?

Okay, so our upbringings weren't so pleasant. That doesn't give us an excuse for continually entertaining thoughts of weakness. "I can't do what she did." "I grew up without parents who cared about me." "My comprehension isn't as good as others people's." "I don't have the energy to get up and do what I need to do for myself."

You can change such thoughts if you really want to. In fact, you can do anything the next man or woman has done, if you would at least try to put forth a sincere effort. "Oh, ye of little faith" (Bible). You possess talents that you have yet to develop and learn to appreciate.

We all have something we are exceptionally good at. It's up to you to discover what it is and perfect it.

Surround yourself with prosperous individuals. Allow them to show you a few things in hopes of it rubbing off. You'll become motivated through witnessing things of substance being put into play. If you look confident, talk with confidence, and act with confidence, you will start to feel much stronger. Try to dress and look as if you consider yourself to be worthy, and people will believe in you without doubt.

You have to jump in someplace, right? Let the first step be a job. It doesn't matter what kind of job it is. Having a job to go to is better than having no job at all. You must learn the ins and outs of your craft. Nothing happens overnight, so you'll have to work your way up from the bottom without complaining. That means coming in on time each morning, with a pleasant disposition and ambition to pull your share of the weight.

All you have to do is think in a creative way. Come up with an original idea. Once you begin to circulate a few good thoughts, soon you'll be able to look at things and come up with different ideas. Ingenuity is all around us. Devote yourself. Stop thinking you can't when everything outside of your personal sickness says that you can. In fact, ban the phrase "I can't" from your mind.

Allow me to provide you with a touch of hope. Poverty is nothing more than a state of mind in which our mental conditions are provided with an opportunity to transform into a physical reality. Poor thoughts equate to a poor environment. A person who has solid thoughts will be able to create prosperity and riches, almost at will. Folks are poor because they refuse to maximize their thoughts and take meaningful action to change their conditions.

Anyone who is mentally wealthy would never permit himself/herself to dwell in poverty for an extended period of time. Think of all the highly successful people who understand the science I am providing you with and who have already extracted themselves from the conditions of the ghetto. Why are so many people poor, you ask? Because they have never been taught the secrets to success.

The more we utilize our power of thought, the clearer our judgement becomes. Good decision-making skills tend to create ways to eliminate problems. Don't give up. No matter how long it may take, stick with it until you come up with a solution.

People talk a good game. You have to ignore certain conversations and focus on your actions. Know with great certainly that you will get out of that dark, miserable hole you've been stuck in for so long. If you're unsure, have the courage to ask for assistance from someone who may know the way.

Refrain from saying negative things about others. Speak of only the good that people do. Believe what I am saying to you. Create positive thoughts and stay in the company of decent people who understand what it means to be successful.

Prosperity will come if you learn to believe in the powers you possess. If, after you have begun to accumulate money, you continue to act irresponsible and poor, sooner rather than later your money will dwindle away. It means very little if you have money but are clueless as to what to do with it. You must respect it.

That entails preventing your impulses from persuading you to be a consumer. Make the money work for you. Don't cater to the urge to buy things you couldn't afford when you didn't have money. Purchase only the things that are essential and strive to create a bigger savings pot than the one you had yesterday.

It doesn't matter how much money people have. If they don't have any respect for how it's supposed to be utilized, they will always find themselves at the bottom, wishing for more.

This is the way of a true entrepreneur. If you do not heed my advice, you will find yourself in the same hole you didn't know how to exit before. Be smart. Make purposeful moves. Use common sense, and always use your ability to be creative in those moments of uncertainty.

You now know that thoughts attract corresponding conditions. If you think and act as though you have money, your environment will reflect such a thought. If you think and act as though you are destitute, your conditions will follow suit. When you know better, you must act accordingly. Get it together, because, honestly, no one cares whether we comfortably float or franticly sink!

JEWEL

Think your way out
of impoverished
conditions.

Who Will Confide in You if You Haven't Learned to Keep a Secret?

Confiding a secret to an unworthy
person is like carrying grain
in a bag with a hole in it.

—ETHIOPIAN PROVERB

THERE COMES A time in life when we must put forth a sincere effort to develop self-restraint and the ability to conceal the things people confide in us and only us.

Indiscretion is not an honorable trait to possess, nor is the person who is acquainted with it worthy of your friendship. Haven't you ever heard "loose lips sink ships"? This conveys a message that sternly warns against confiding in people who do not recognize the value of keeping things strictly to themselves, and it also makes you aware that it's only a matter of time before what was meant to remain unknown to others becomes the cause of your plans being ruined.

Avoid the habit of telling people your business. Keep things to yourself. Why do you think you are always the last person to find out what's going on? Most likely it's because you do too much talking. Everyone seems to enjoy talking about everything that has absolutely nothing to do with them. There is no excuse for why you feel a need to repeat what someone has told you in total confidence. What right-minded person would feel inclined to trust someone who has proven unable to keep his/her lips sealed? Certainly no one with character.

At this stage of development, you should at least be familiar with a few methods for controlling your desires. In particular, the desire to reveal to others what you have been told or what you have overheard. Such a desire needs to be checked and well-guarded.

When a person divulges things of a sensitive nature to you or shows you a few things that aren't meant for "anyone else," never mention a single word to anyone! Forget the conversation ever took place.

How do you fight such an urge? It's simple: when you witness something or catch wind of things the average person considers to be juicy information, suppress the inclination to speak of them. If it was your business, would you feel comfortable with others discussing it? No? Well, that pretty much settles it. There should be no reason why you feel a need to discuss things that have such little value to you. It's called practicing self-restraint. Wrong is wrong, remember? The nature of such an urge is to blab to anyone who is willing to lend an ear. Fight the temptation intensely until it goes away. The pressure of desire will always try to persuade us all to talk a lot more than we need to. You have the discipline. Resist the temptation by telling yourself, "I'm in control." The urge to discuss the things that shouldn't even be on your radar will quickly go away.

A person who possesses tact will neither accidently nor intentionally divulge his/her secrets to others. It's important for us to learn how to keep our business to ourselves. Do not make the mistake of thinking you can trust everyone to protect your personal secrets, because for the right price or a chance to save themselves from possible punishment, some people will never hesitate to give up everything they know. In their minds, it's a dog-eat-dog world, and from their rational points of view, it's either you or them who must be the sacrificial lamb. It's not a mystery as to who becomes dinner. What are you even doing discussing anything with people whose souls are shallow? Have you not learned anything at all? These are the people who are really wolves dressed in sheep's clothing. It is not okay to accept anything at all from them. Their smiles are meant to put you at ease.

This is the reason why you must resist the temptation to tell your most intimate secrets to total strangers, friends, and family. Learn to keep a few things to yourself. At least 90 percent of the people we think we know will prove to be nothing close to what they will have us believe. If you really must tell someone something, let it go no further than from your mouth to God's ears. This way you don't have to worry about receiving the short end of the stick.

Never be remiss of the fact that everyone has someone they feel comfortable confiding in. When we choose to discuss a secret with a friend, there should be no doubt that he/she will instinctively feel an urge to tell a person whom they trust. The circle will continue to perpetuate until what you believe to have been a secret is actually now everyone's business. You will then become consumed with worries, for there is a strong likelihood that what you have initially revealed to someone in secret may come back to haunt you in the worst way.

Has it for one second crossed your mind that perhaps the friend of your friend may not approve of you very much and therefore cannot wait for a golden opportunity to reveal what he/she knows about your personal affairs? Think, my friend, think.

> Whenever you are to do a thing,
> though it can never be known but
> to yourself, ask yourself how you
> would act were all the world looking
> at you, and act accordingly.
>
> **—THOMAS JEFFERSON**

You don't have to tell people everything you know. Take your secrets to the grave with you. There is no telling when someone will feel a need to betray you for a reason that will always be an aggravating mystery to you. The scariest thing about telling everyone your business is the fact you won't have the slightest clue as to what direction the betrayal comes from.

Guess what? Sometimes the most painful heart-aches come from those who live in the same castle as us. Yes, that's right, family. Those who are the closest to us. You will never see it coming. Consider the mindset of the spouse who may feel as though you have been less than honest, and now the time has arisen for you to pay the Pied Piper. Don't you dare cry if you cannot stand the consequences of what you have done.

Those who we love the most sometimes innocently, or purposefully, tell our secrets to others who could care less about what we think. It's nothing personal. They don't know how to mind their own business, and certainly, they can't wait to find an angle that will help them to benefit from what they have learned.

> There are no secrets amongst the
> weak. Once you open your mouth
> to reveal something of importance,
> it becomes inevitable that the
> world will soon know too.
>
> **—RAYMOND POWELL**

Perfect your character and act as if you know a few things.

> If a stranger understands a town's
> affairs, it is because of a citizen.
>
> **—AKAN PROVERB**

JEWEL

Try speaking less and
listening a little more,
there's always truth
to be found in jest.

—SHAWN TURNER

How Good Does Your Self-Esteem Make You Feel?

If you have no self confidence in yourself you are twice defeated in the race of life. With confidence you have won even before you have started.

—HON. MARCUS MOSIAH GARVEY

SELF-ESTEEM IS THE fuel that permits us to glow with self-love, self-respect, a balanced pride, and a show of admiration for who we are. It is a rewarding confidence extended to our willingness to walk proudly without conceit or offense to others. It is an internal richness that offers a position amongst the stars. It is an uncompromising faith in your personal values.

Self-esteem is what emboldens us to take step after step after step with a merciful smile. No wonder there are always a few who seem to be easily irritated after we have arrived with grace.

It is perfectly normal for you to feel a desire to

enjoy things being about you for once. The indispensable time that's utilized for pampering yourself: Visits to the beauty salon. A few shopping sprees. The purchasing of fragrances that complement the uniqueness of your personality and the strength of your soul. Vacations that encourage you to unwind and have a little fun. A quiet evening out on the town or maybe just some time alone with the serenity of your thoughts. These are a few things that can help to promote a healthy self-esteem.

Allow me to tell you something about self-esteem. No one can provide you with the real deal. It is something you will have to develop for yourself. It is encompassing. At the heart of it, you naturally exist just the way you are. It will never attempt to convince you that you are in need of anyone or anything, aside from the help of the Almighty, to validate your worth. Who else can provide you with such an infectious smile? How about your genuine ability to complement people every day? You have a natural disposition that entices others to comment on the sweetness of your personality, and this is what a healthy self-esteem looks like.

Despite what is going on in your life, hold your head up. Walk your walk and have a delightful appreciation for who you are. When you smile, the world will create a smile to return to you. Why would it not? After all, your life has valuable meaning. There is no conceivable value that is more substantial than that of a healthy mind and soul. Always love yourself unconditionally!

 **JEWEL**

Self-esteem is what fuels that gracious walk of yours. It's what permits you to hold your head up with a smile.

–KAREEM MOREFIELD

An Apology Costs Very Little

An apology can sometimes be
difficult to put in words, but when
we can find the courage to choose
healing over continued pain, we
increase the value of our heart.

—VAUGHN WRIGHT

LIFE WILL NEVER be devoid of personal mistakes, offensive words, unnecessary criticisms, or biased judgements. Humans err every day; in particular, when we are not on our best behavior. We often say and do things we do not mean. As I've said, sometimes unintentionally, those who care about us are the ones who end up hurt the most. That doesn't exclude those we have only known for a short period of time from becoming victims of our misspoken words or inconsiderate actions. Words that are poorly spoken and actions that are distastefully committed are exceedingly hard to retract. The question then becomes whether or not we possess the courage to step up and offer an apology to those we have offended.

When we're able to admit we have made a mistake and sincerely apologize for the pain we caused others, it becomes a true testament of our humanity. We become more valuable, not only to ourselves, but to those who have love for us. Yes, sometimes it is extremely difficult to prevent your pride from getting in the way of doing the right thing, but this is what true courage looks like.

In our moments of ignorance, if someone is offended by our rash behavior or words that were unthoughtfully articulated, find the strength to say, "I apologize." It takes nothing away from who you are. It does, however, offer an opportunity to receive admiration and appreciation from others for your ability to admit when you were wrong.

Forget about what the selfish and miserable people will think of you. Apologize because you know better. Not everyone will be the bigger person, one who can admit they were wrong, but that's not your concern.

When someone stops talking to you because of something they have said or did that was wrong, be the bigger person and initiate an apology that's coated with true forgiveness. If people have an ounce of compassion in their hearts, they will immediately feel horrible for not doing what they know deep down inside they should have done first.

The vast majority of people go through life burdened with a heavy heart because their false pride won't allow them to clear the air between them and a relationship that was worth salvaging.

Inevitably, you will encounter many people who

allow their pride to dictate their actions and speech. If only they knew how silly they appear in the eyes of the unpretentious.

When you apologize for the things you have done wrong, people will be more inclined to happily forgive you and welcome you closer to their hearts. Treat folks the way you want to be treated, and that includes offering an apology whenever you offend others.

JEWEL

Apologizing when you are in the wrong is a form of therapy for the soul.

Dispense Justice Righteously

The true seeker of truth never loses hope. The true seeker of real justice never tires. A farmer does not stop planting seeds just because of the failure of one crop. Success is born of trying and trying again. Truth must seek justice. Justice must seek the truth. When justice triumphs, truth will reign on earth.

– NGŨGĨ WA THIONG'O

TAKE A GOOD look at yourself. The qualities that make you a decent person have begun to embolden your righteousness. No one can say for certain exactly when you will be called upon to exercise your ability to be just and impartial.

Impartiality entails having absolutely no favorites and at all times remaining unaffected or swayed by your emotions when judging a factual dispute.

Being an excellent listener is mandatory. You must

be confident that your sense of hearing will not fail you, for every detail must be heard correctly.

- Logical thinker. It is imperative that you are able to place the facts together logically, in order, to arrive at a reliable conclusion. No guesstimating.
- Observation. Your ability to observe must be unrelenting.

These are the ingredients for justice. She has no biases, no preconceived opinions, and certainly no concern for your status in life. Right is right and wrong is wrong! Never tamper with such a delicate balance.

Should you become a dispenser of justice, never let it be written: "You were partial on your scale of balance, a selective listener when it came to hearing correctly, illogical in your thinking, and constantly disregarded your observations."

Permit the world to rejoice in your ability to remain unbiased, despite cultural, financial, or social differences between the people of one race—the human race!

 **JEWEL**

It's the love of justice that strengthens the soul.

—ASALE NYANSATUMI

Gossiping Is for the Weak-Minded

A gossip betrays in confidence, but
a trustworthy man keeps a secret.

–PROVERBS 11:13

WHAT UNCOMPLIMENTARY CON-
VERSATION are we discussing today?
Allow me to guess—rumors you think are
juicy enough to enthrall the world. Shame on you! Gossiping and being nosy are closely akin, as they both tell
a tale of nasty habits with debilitating consequences.

Entirely too much energy and brain power is
wasted indulging in vile conversation that in no way,
shape, or form pertains to us. Is there not something
else you could be doing with your time, instead of listening and then running to repeat the secrets of others
to those who have no business knowing? Why would
you travel down such a dark road? The information
you're revealing to others is nothing more than unso-
licited revelations, which means that you not only have
a serious problem with being too loquacious, but you

also have no qualms about whose business you divulge. How disappointing, and to consider the fact that you weren't even pressured into revealing what someone told you in total confidence is even more alarming.

People who sit around talking about others are full of bitterness. They find great pleasure in discussing the faults and failures of those around them.

A person's criticism of you, even when it proves to be ludicrous, will always be scrutinized by those who have a false sense of being emphatically correct. These are the same folks who will smile in your face and then reveal your personal secrets faster than it takes for you to confide in them. For the amount of pain they've caused you to bear, you would have been better off to have kept your secrets to yourself. You have no one to blame other than yourself. Certainly you knew from the start that such people were scandalous by nature. Don't trust so easily.

A person who is a gossip will talk about you out of jealousy because he/she is envious or for no other reason than having hatred for you.

....
A perverse man stirs up dissension,
and a gossip separates close friends.
—PROVERBS 16:28
....

Gossiping robs us of potential while our egos are constantly in search of ways to help us feel important in the eyes of those who couldn't care less about us.

Don't be a scurrilous individual. If your associates attempt to spread rumors or discuss the private affairs of those who you're cool with, prove you have a backbone and abruptly cut the conversation short. There is nothing to be gained from listening to someone gossip about other people, especially those who you care about. Such demeaning conversations are indicative of a serious weakness on your behalf, a weakness that will hamper a recovering heart from attaining self-discipline and knowing what it means to be a person of principles.

> Do not let unwelcome talk come
> out of your mouth, but only what
> is helpful for building others up
> according to their needs, that
> may benefit those who listen.
>
> **–EPHESIANS 4:29**

Avoid permitting yourself to be used as a sounding board for those who can't help finding a need to criticize everyone other than themselves. You needn't feel embarrassed about having to tell the people doing the criticizing that they should discuss their grievances with the people they have a problem with.

If you ever have an issue with someone and feel as though the situation is weighing heavy on your heart, let it be aired with those you have a problem with and no one else. You possess courage and good taste; act like it. Speak up and say what you feel. There are no points to be gained for attempting to make others appear to be petty, while in the back of your mind you really think you have caused yourself to look good in the eyes of other people. By chance, you just may be gossiping to someone who is a friend of the person you're talking about or who could be playing along just to see what your character is really made of.

Anytime you or someone else speaks less than favorably about other people, it's gossiping! Such talk equates to nothing more than a bunch of half-truths and sordid lies.

Develop a distaste for listening to those who speak of things that do not pertain to them. The logic is pretty simple: if you permit people to gossip about others while in your company, tomorrow they will feel very comfortable gossiping about you.

Gossiping is a vicious act that is committed by those who lack self-worth. Their only true intent is to ruin the good name of those they seek to psychologically and emotionally destroy.

....

If you damage the character of
another, you damage your own.

—YORUBA PROVERB

....

 **JEWEL**

A person who gossips is insecure about themselves.

—SALIMAH YOUNGBLOOD

Trust Isn't To Be Extended to Everyone

....

Where trust breaks down,
peace breaks down.

—AFRICAN PROVERB

....

TRUST IS A genuine code comprised of honesty, morals, uncompromising strength, and reliability, all insightfully woven into the structure of our genetics. It is untainted blood flowing through the hearts of those who feel as if they should be able to confidently lean on a special person without having to worry about disloyalty, deceitfulness, or the possibility of treacherous violations. A willingness to offer our trust is not only proof of our selflessness; it is a raw testament of the compassion and faith that is held so dear to us.

The unreliableness of those who often show signs of an undisciplined character will never amount to anything more than what it is. Please attempt to find the words to express why you feel so inclined to trust a person who is unwilling to cultivate his/her intellect.

You have God as your ultimate provider, the main source who has warned us all of the toils that secretly lie within the hearts of those who are disappointingly unsound. Your struggles, your blessings, your joyful tears, your undaunted spirit, and your elegant nature should never permit you to give your trust to anyone who is no more than average. When we can begin to respectfully understand our personal value and start living life from the driver's seat, as opposed to the back seat, those questionably dark clouds hovering above will gradually roll away to make way for the sight of beautiful sunshine.

Before we can entertain thoughts of trusting others, they will have to prove their worth. For starters, are their internal scars consistent with their professed pains? All you have to do is listen closely. Observe a little better. What have they been through that would prevent them from recklessly trampling on the gift of your trust? There is entirely too much at stake for you to risk believing in someone who doesn't care anything about being reciprocal, someone whose thoughts are more like dangerously overhung icicles. A true friendship is forever.

Forget all the small talk. What do their actions speak of? Sure, we could all use someone to converse with, but slow it down a minute. There's no rush to act as if you're dying of thirst.

....

The humility of royalty never
displays signs of being in a haste
for anything accept for prayer.

—RAYMOND POWELL

....

Before placing your confidence in other people, take some time to observe how they interact with others. Are they polite, respectful, and capable of flying under the radar? Are their spirits worthy of mingling with your wisdom? Do they speak much? See if you can identify more honorable qualities than unpleasant weaknesses. If you cannot, there is no reason to invest your time in getting to know them better. You certainly know a few things.

Hold on to your trust until you are convinced that the right person is deserving of your friendship or at least worthy of a closer inspection. Don't be so quick to trust everyone you meet. Be slightly cautious! Not everyone is who they portray themselves to be.

 **JEWEL**

Trust selectively.

It Helps To Be Resilient

....

It is the deformation of our sincerest
thoughts that hinder us from
developing a resilient spirit.

–JUSTIN MITCHELL

....

WE ALL ARE bound to make a few mistakes, but the more we crave intellectually, the less likely we'll suffer for long. Keep on striving. If something isn't working, don't be afraid to change a few things. Stop being so hard on yourself. You are going to go through a few harsh realities. Realities that may cause you to question the integrity of your purpose. Realities that will cause others to be envious of you. Realities that will persuade you to consider whether your best is ever good enough. Don't you dare spend too much time worrying about the constant bombardment of disparaging remarks made by those who would never qualify to walk a single day in your shoes. It isn't until we stop trying that we noticeably begin dying!

Misplaced frustration for our shortcomings is nothing more than an overreaction. It's nothing to get all bent out of shape about. Get up and put a little antibacterial ointment on your scrapes and bruises, and try again. But this time, arm yourself with the lessons of your errors.

Find it in your heart to define and demonstrate excellence while in the face of misfortunes. This is how resilience reveals itself, in hopes that we may choose to grasp the mettle that will solidify our ability to bounce back.

Be unrelenting in your reluctance to identify in any way with giving up or creating bogus excuses for why you think you cannot do what needs to be done. Those of us who know what it is to be resilient gather unfathomable strength from, not only the hardships we have personally endured, but from the tragedies of those who came way before our time.

Psychological hurdles should never be a factor when you're trying to determine what the best course is for confronting life's circumstances. It's not in our nature to be weak! To shrivel up and act cowardly when contemplating how best to defy the difficulties standing before us.

In a nutshell, those who find themselves trapped in a pit of abhorrence with nothing at all, except for their sanity, creative thoughts, and the courage to aspire to something much, much greater than what they can physically see, are the real embodiment of what it is to be resilient.

When you have nothing more than two dollars to your name, but without complaints you feel a strong desire to get back on top and prove you are worthy of being a winner, that is resilient. Being at the bottom of anything affords you only two options: one, continue to dwell there and drown in self-pity while accepting handouts, or two, have confidence in what you know you can do. You are able to shoot for the horizon with ambitions for accomplishing your objectives.

Basking in poverty and the daily hassles and stress that stem from less-than-favorable circumstances is no good for anyone who is able to visualize the concept of heaven while here on earth.

So many of us come from broken homes that have robbed us of knowing the love, joy, and experience of being raised by two beautiful parents, as opposed to only one. Yes, it can be disturbing, but who with such great strength cries over spilled milk? In life, your grievances should never serve as a deterrent that can prevent you from realizing the taste of success of any magnitude.

To be resilient speaks volumes about the strength of your mind, the respectability of your might, and the elasticity of your resolve to keep on keeping on. No one has the slightest clue as to what you have been through, the unpleasant sacrifices you've had to make for God knows how long, and the willpower it has taken for you to fight every single day and overcome what seemed to be dire impossibilities. Shame on them. If they only knew the power you really possess.

When your moment arrives to mentor those who have inspirational potential, do so with an abundance of love and concern that will resonate inside of the support group in which you are a part of. Be moderately protective with the intent to help lessen the risks and stress that tend to quickly build up inside of dysfunctional environments. How will you know when you have been successful with developing pupils who are resilient? They will do without having to be asked to do, and when they get it done, it will be with a spirit of pure gratitude.

Each and every morning you are blessed to awaken, confidently exclaim, "I am a survivor and a real winner!" It has been rumored that we will not amount to anything more than screw ups and total failures. We must prove them wrong, but only after we have sincerely challenged ourselves and have achieved something worth being proud of.

Learn to be defiant in the face of the obstacles that are in your way. You can make it if you learn to refuse to go in the same direction that everyone else has gone in. Following the masses is easy, but being a leader takes great courage. Make your own path by utilizing the power of your own thoughts, and then you too shall be considered resilient.

 JEWEL

Show people what it means to be resilient.

—DONALD EUBANKS

Saying "Yes" Is More Soothing

....

He who has no manners does
not care about others.

—SWAHILI PROVERB

....

SINCE EMBARKING ON the road to refinement, it has become incumbent upon us to elevate our level of manners and respect for others. When conversing with people and a question is asked of you that warrants giving an affirmative response, do not be hesitant to answer by saying yes. It shows that you not only have a good character, but you also have the utmost respect for the people you're addressing.

When we truly value the privilege of sitting amongst personable older people, it requires us to answer them by clearly saying, "Yes, ma'am," or, "Yes, sir"! No matter what position in life older people find themselves occupying, always remember that we owe them respect. We have not lived long enough to witness half of the things elders have seen. The ailing woman who doesn't walk so well anymore is worthy of your respect. Back in her day, she was an ambassador to the country and her reputation was impeccable. Oh, now you see her in a different light, do you?

Consider this scenario: The ol' timer who you look down on because every day he's too intoxicated to hold his head up high is worthy of your respect! In 1954, federal agents raided his goodwill store and confiscated six million dollars. It was secretively stashed in the basement by someone he had once helped get back on his feet. A kid was in the process of stealing clothes that folks had donated when he stumbled upon the fortune. He ran home and told his father, who happened to be an FBI agent. Turns out the old man who owned the store never even knew. Uncle Sam delicately extracted the large sums of money, and no charges were ever filed for tax evasion. Go figure!

No one had any idea that the old man had dedicated his life to secretively helping people. The man who placed the large sum of money in the basement was dying of cancer. He refused to leave it to his family because they had no respect for anyone. He remembered the generosity of the ol' timer and deeply admired how he was always respectful to everyone he met. He had a natural love for helping people in any way that he could. Respect will take you further than you could ever imagine.

Always leave others with the impression that you are more than average and have something extraordinary going on in your heart. Saying yes could never take away from who you are. If anything, it gives the person who taught you respect a chance to admire your style and credits your character with a pleasantness that will leave others wanting just a little bit more. Look in the mirror to familiarize yourself with saying yes. Notice how sweet it sounds. It's like honey rolling off your tongue.

The next time someone asks you a question, especially an elder, respond by saying yes. Pay close attention to how people look at you with astonishment. Good manners are hard to come by nowadays. Make the word "yes" part of your daily vocabulary.

> Having a taste for good manners
> will cause you to be remembered,
> even when you're convinced that
> you have been forgotten.
>
> **—NIA TATE**

JEWEL

Show them your higher self!

The Power of
Our Words

WE MUST BE extremely careful about what we say and how we choose to say it. The words we birth are infused with tremendous power. Power that constantly demonstrates the life force of things that are not apparent.

What we put into the universe verbally will not return void. Our words have vibratory powers capable of transforming spoken words into attraction. Those who continuously speak hatred attract hate. If you continuously speak of wealth, you will ultimately attract it.

Once you understand that words have life, you must be careful of what you speak of. What goes around comes back around. If you wish harm on someone, sooner or later, harm will become attracted to you.

When you wish prosperity upon others, know that you are wishing prosperity upon yourself. Have you never known the influence of a motivational speaker? What about the power of prayer? We reap what we sow.

> Even as I have seen, they
> that plow iniquity, and sow
> wickedness, reap the same.
>
> **– J O B 4 : 8**

What do you think affirmations are about? I will explain. They are about confidently speaking aloud what you would like to bring into existence. Be careful what you wish for; you just may receive it. Once words are spoken, they develop a momentum all their own. A life force is behind the words we speak, and when they are set in motion, there is absolutely no chance of recalling them.

Nonverbal words are just as powerful. Can you recall a time when you were thinking about someone and, almost instantaneously, you received a phone call or text from that person? That wasn't a coincidence. Welcome to the power of telepathy. The misunderstood "coincidence" relating to telepathy is nothing other than the Law of Attraction. All actions, all things, and all words fulfill the law of its being. Remember cause and effect? An effect is nothing more than the direct result of the cause. For example, inharmony on the outside is an indication of there being inharmony mentally. If you wish people happiness, the same will come back to you, provided you do not entertain thoughts or speak words that will neutralize the law.

Words misspoken cause pain; angrily directed, they are insurmountably damaging; sincerely whispered, they have the potential to inspire hope. But when words are verbalized with compassion, it is a reminder that someone truly cares about the condition of your life.

Recognize the potential of your words. They have unbelievable power to either create or destroy. Speak with kindness and truth so that you may become a recipient of the same.

> Death and life are in the power
> of the tongue; and they that love
> it shall eat the fruit thereof.
>
> **– PROVERBS 18:21**

When we sow, no matter if it is through the words we speak, the thoughts we occupy, or our actions, we set something in motion. Reaping is the payment of what we have sown. It usually entails facing some form of consequences for our actions, regardless of whether our intentions were good or bad.

The world is full of people who thrive on being negative. Pay no attention to those who have nothing positive to say. The words spewed from the mouths of those who feel intimidated by you can only sting if you acknowledge their existence. Keep doing what you're doing and confidently smile your smile. After all, words are only words.

....

If you do not fear the battle
front, you do not fear the front
where words are weapons.

–AKAN PROVERB

....

 **JEWEL**

Be extremely careful about what you say.

Life Is Perfectly Balanced for a Reason

WHAT IS TRUE balance? Balance is the harmonious stability of all things. It is a precise accuracy that guarantees indistinguishable proportions to opposing sides. Take, for instance, justice. Lady Justice wears a blindfold that signifies her oath to be unbiased in all of her judgements, regardless of a person's ethnicity, gender, or social standing. If so much as the weight of an atom is discriminately moved from one side of the scale to the other, what once was meant to be impartial suddenly becomes prejudicial. Who can be confident of receiving their "just due" if the scales of justice constantly function as if they require recalibrating?

Nature is masterfully balanced. During the fall season, trees begin to lose their luster. Their leaves have a preordained time and purpose, after which time they shrivel up and replenish the floor of the earth. The birds migrate south for warmer conditions during the winter months. Bears instinctively awaken from hibernation in search of food during the spring, and the attractive, colorful bloom of many flowers flourishes in the summer due to a delicate balance provided by Mother Nature. It is a balance we fail to see as being important.

While walking the path of life, we tend to take a great deal of things for granted. Our overblown egos, false pride, layered excuses, and pathological distortion of the truth prevent us from humbling ourselves long enough to think about what life in someone else's shoes might be like. Balance is not solely about discovering ways to manage your life free of daily complications. It is looking outside of yourself to acknowledge those who have no immediate alternative for wearing shoes with holes in them. Surely their condition is worse than yours, but how many times did the imbalance in your heart cause you to intentionally overlook their status? Be honest. Balance is about doing something to help enlighten those who are mentally depleted. It is providing food for those who cannot gather the strength to secure sustenance on their own. We cannot continue to take, take, take without honestly pondering the balance of what must be returned.

When you can grasp the concept of an equality balance, then you can stop wasting time worrying about what pair of shoes is required to travel down a particular path in life. You won't have to agonize over headaches, heartaches, or the mental instability of your soul. Ah, yes. Now you might be able to peacefully enjoy the gratification of a spiritual balance. The man or woman who strives daily to see the goodness in others and who can appreciate the generosity bestowed upon him/her, regardless of the selfishness of those who pretend to care, is a person who understands what balance means.

Nothing exists that has not been provided with perfect balance by the creator.

A false balance is abomination to the lord; but a just weight is his highlight.

–PROVERB 11:1

Let every thought that you entertain, every action that you take, and every emotion that you feel have complete balance to it.

J E W E L

Without balance there is no stability.

The Scorn of Betrayal

Nothing hurts worse than experiencing
a betrayal by the one person whom
you thought would be loyal forever.

–JAMES E. BALLARD

BETRAYAL IS THE ultimate violation of one's trust. It is an inexcusable wrong to those who have been taught to never imitate treacherous people.

To those of us who live a life of unwavering faithfulness, betrayal by a companion can come stomping in the form of infidelity. I'm sorry, but some people will not have regard for your love. To those who know what it means to be truthful and abide by the rules, betrayal will sometimes appear mysteriously cloaked in what seems to be true, but it is actually nothing more than an alluring falseness. For those who have vowed to patiently endure your hardships, having a sudden change of heart for no apparent reason can, and often does, equate to betrayal. Not everyone is equipped to stand strong while adversity passes by. It all depends on how much you have mentally and emotionally invested.

Say you have a wonderful boyfriend. You love him and you're pretty sure he feels the same. God forbid, but you become really, really sick. He cannot deal with it and up and leaves you—betrayal. He had you believe you guys were going to be married and grow old together; now, because he doesn't want to take care of you, he's gone!

If you have found yourself to be the recipient of such a deplorable act, it may be time for introspection. How was this person permitted to get so close and how did you fail to detect any warning signs at all? What prevented you from listening to the wisdom of your heart? Your intuition? That gut feeling! Whether we're dealing with family or friends, we must always possess the courage to shine a teaching light on the flawed characteristics and actions of those who are dear to us. Those we love sometimes have minor, or major, flaws. We must possess the courage to let them know when they are wrong. If we don't, ultimately, their bad habits can lead to betrayal. This is how you're supposed to treat those you care about.

You'll come across a few folks who will enjoy screaming, "Death before dishonor!" It actually sounds pretty comforting, but what is to be said of the friend who has found himself/herself unable to resist crossing the boundaries of your trust? What about the certitude you tried to extend before that friend maliciously proved he/she should have never been treated as family in the first place?

Even those who claim not to betray are capable of doing so. Say you have a tattoo, Death Before Betrayal, which implies you would rather die before embarking upon a road of disgrace. Okay, cool. But what could possibly justify your deceitful ways? The lies that effortlessly ooze from your lips each time they open to speak? What about the time your friend thought you were a responsible and solid individual who was worthy of entrusting with the daily operation of his business, but then you somehow managed to conjure up a deceptive ploy that allowed you to maneuver yourself into becoming the sole proprietor, without consent? Is that not betrayal?

Acknowledging and adhering to the values of being honorable is a pleasure that not many people cherish anymore. See, you must first know what true friendship is before completely trusting with so much confidence. You should be acquainted with the comforts of a balanced partnership long before confiding from the depths of your soul. You must truly understand what it means to share with others before expecting to receive in any capacity whatsoever. We all must learn how to, not only lead people correctly, but to modestly glow in their approval, long before we can become a shining star worth admiration. In that single star, you can be certain that its light will never lead anyone astray, reveal the secrets of the heavens, or violate the confidence of the galaxies. That, my friend, is loyalty without so much as a hint of betrayal.

Frequently, we find ourselves overlooking small violations of those who have been given our friendship; despite how minor the violations may be, such infractions serve as indicators of people not being worthy of our loyalty. Ignoring such warnings can cause us to end up on the losing end of the stick every single time.

Hurt? Yes. Emotionally scarred? Possibly forever. But the lesson gained should never permit you to repeat the same mistake twice! Oftentimes, self-interest finds a way to persuade folks to abandon their allegiance with you, and well, I assume you know the moral to the story.

Never, under any circumstances, accept someone's excuse for why he/she betrayed you. Should a situation come to light that causes you to question an element of a person's loyalty, know with great certainty that you have just perceived a transgression waiting to occur.

 **JEWEL**

When you are playing with a dog, do not ever forget to keep a stick within reach.

—AKAN PROVERB

We Are All Unique in Our Own Way

The way you think. The depths of your creativity. The strength to patiently observe your creations evolve. It is all a reflection of your uniqueness.

—LA'SHANDA CRAWFORD

YOU POSSESS QUALITIES that naturally arouse the curiosity of others. Qualities that, if embraced, have the potential to propel you further than you could ever imagine. Let's count the ways: One, you have a mind and a heart that is waiting to become one with your spirit. Only through following the wisdom of your soul can your heart be guided to explore the healing effects of your spirit. Don't accept this truth because it sounds good. Take a minute to analyze the facts, and you will personally see how gifted you truly are. Two, you were blessed to awaken this morning with a new perspective. You know a few more things than you knew yesterday! Three, you are a survivor. That in itself empowers you to continue moving forward in search of something more meaningful. Life shouldn't be viewed as a task of drudgery and confusion. It's supposed to be full of patience, understanding, and a manifestation of your mind. Four, you have experience. Relax. Stop worrying so much. We all have minor flaws that can sometimes be difficult to manage. Work on them before they become offensively problematic to others. Five, you have a pleasant gift that permits you to articulate your thoughts and your feelings. Not everyone is capable of expressing the way they feel or effortlessly discussing their past afflictions, ambitions, or interests. You have a talented voice. Let it be clearly heard so those who aren't as fortunate may have a chance to benefit from the deliverance of your message.

Very few people are able to immediately identify what qualifies them to be unique. Your genius has been waiting for the longest time to be discovered. Make no mistake about it: it's in your blood. It was etched in your soul many generations ago. Can't you feel it? Shhh. You must be silent to help it evolve. Your uniqueness is the key to unlocking your hidden talents. You have a competitive hunger for at least one thing that no one else can do the way that you do it. Some place deep within, your potential is being held captive. Maybe it's being suppressed due to procrastination, self-sabotaging, too much buffoonery, fear of what others may think, or simply, because you aren't conscious of what's been secretly known all along—you are a genius!

Your spirit is extremely unique. It has a natural yearning to soar in search of discovering what life is really about. Contrary to popular opinion, it wants nothing more than for you to search and become acquainted with portions of yourself that have long awaited to welcome you home. There is absolutely no time to lose. Arrogance, pettiness, stubbornness, vindictiveness, and the brilliance of our genius don't do so well with being complementary to each other. Good and bad could never coexist.

Please don't shy away or become agitated. Come closer. This is something important that needs to be shared with you. Being a genius is not strictly reserved for chemists, architects, surgeons, anatomists, or educators with inspirational minds. A genius is defined in a number of ways. A wise man once said:

It is genius to know what to say and exactly when to say it. It is genius to have creative energy that is capable of formulating the appropriate strategy at a moment that is fitting. It is genius to possess a spiritual ability to intellectually assemble a vessel that may guide attentive people to the annals of history. But, it is ingenious to identify, and fully understand the necessity of providing mental nourishment to those who have been persecuted without reason!

Mr. and Mrs. Ezell, the founders of Sweet Homes Healthcare—Mr. Ezell was raised in the ghetto and went on to become a multimillionaire—take an appreciative look at yourselves. Your courage to defeat the odds is commendable. Your persistence to complete the task you began while forging your accomplishments is truly enlightening. You have managed to amass the wisdom needed to exfoliate the skin of the ghetto, while remaining loyal to your passion for reaching back to coach those who dream of someday following your steps.

I honor you for having exquisite taste, inspirational courage, and a love for not forgetting where you came from. To think of how you pursued and delicately extracted your dreams, all while residing in the midst of daily chaos, is nothing less than extraordinary. It is my pleasure to welcome your induction to the newly created "Hall of Great Geniuses"!

Oprah Winfrey's rise from muddied waters to arrive at a prosperous new beginning was genius. President Barrack H. Obama's genius was discovered in his exuberant charisma; such charisma hasn't been seen since Hannibal the Great successfully traversed the Alps. Bill Gates's philanthropic spirit, which slightly outshined Steve Jobs' metamorphic contributions, was genius. Can you imagine the power of two geniuses collaborating to form such a powerful conglomerate? Wow! That's pretty amazing.

Tyler Perry, artistic genius. Shawn Carter, musical genius. Queen Latifah, sophisticated genius. Steve Harvey, alluring genius. Russell Simons, celestially driven genius. Denzel Washington, teaching genius! Maya Angelou, poetic genius. I thank all of you for your selfless sacrifices and countless contributions to humanity. It is my sole pleasure to officially welcome your induction into the Hall of Great Geniuses.

Today, pupils, your way of thinking, as it pertains to your creativity and the consciousness of your actions, is very different. You have evolved to a level of winning, which in itself is proof of your uniqueness.

Extend your hand to those who possess a

complementary soul that's absent a desire to blow out your candle in an attempt to highlight their own exaggerated unselfishness. Some folks really have selflessly chosen to help enhance the flame that belongs to you. Is that not unique in its own right?

....

Brilliant minds create ways to
prosper, in spite of the annoyance
of their current struggles.

—MICHAEL CRAWFORD

....

Being uniquely creative is a personal trait that welcomes others to commend your accomplishments with an exclamation point and a genuine smile. Your generosity equates to their receptiveness. Their hunger to learn matches your willingness to feed their minds. Your genius, their quest to explore greatness. Their perceptions, your truthfulness. Your cautious strides, their endless possibilities. Their response to fear, your thoughtful judgements. Your compassion, their eagerness to seek just a little bit more. Their creativity plus your creativity together represent the foundation of something that is bound to be celebrated. It's all a validation for the necessity of an interchanging bond between graceful people who seek an enriched ground to exist upon. Our purest ideas have always been covered with genius, and that alone qualifies each one of us to be exceptionally unique!

JEWEL

Life would be
unbelievably boring
if we were all the
same. Starting today,
celebrate your
personal uniqueness.

Procrastinators Will Always Miss Opportunities

....

If you continually create excuses
for why you have yet to do what
needs to be done, chances are, the
task may never be completed.

—SHAYNÉ FRISBY

....

IT HAS BEEN suggested that procrastination is one of many crippling tools that lurk around the devil's workshop. It comes with a contagious comfort. One that implies pleasure is received each time good people are found delaying what needs to be done.

Time is of the essence. It will not stand still while we attempt to create excuses for our laziness. In those precious seconds of delaying, opportunities are casually passing by without any curiosity whatsoever for how you may have utilized what you missed out on. Sounds fair, especially when attention is drawn to the fact that you have a really bad habit of pretending you enjoy hindering progress. No? Then try explaining why whenever someone asks you to do something, it takes what feels like forever before you get around to accomplishing the task? Perhaps if you weren't so quick to agree to accommodating every request placed before you, then there wouldn't be any pressure on you to show and prove.

When we commit ourselves to do something, we must immediately come through. Ol' Lady Procrastination has a way of causing us to become complacent. It's as if we fail to see anything wrong with suspending the pressing chores of today until we run into an urgency for completing the same chores tomorrow. If you procrastinate doing the things that you're supposed to do, it will leave an un-erasable mark on your character. Are you really going to keep delaying everything? Certainly this is not the mentality of a person who is confident in his/her abilities and welcoming of new challenges.

Procrastinating can cause people to distance themselves from you. Why would anyone who has their priorities in order feel inclined to associate with a man or woman who has a habit of overlooking things that need to be done? Excuses are for the weak. If someone was to have faith in you, it would only be a short period of time before you began to put off things you are expected to do, in hopes of the next person coming along to complete them. Now, in your mind, you have to create another excuse for why you didn't tend to your responsibilities. Thinkers don't procrastinate; they immediately get the job done! For, in those precious moments of executing your duties, an idea may be discovered that may change your life forever.

> The less one has to do, the less
> time one finds to do it in. One
> yawns, one procrastinates, one can
> do it when one will, and therefore
> one seldom does it at all.
>
> **—EARL OF CHESTERFIELD**

What are you waiting for? Show those who you have dealings with that you can be depended upon and don't have a problem with immediately tending to your obligations. When you make a decision to do something, regardless if it's for you or others, do your absolute best to get it done without resignation.

> Never put off till tomorrow,
> what you can do today.
>
> **—ENGLISH PROVERB**

Work towards your goals with a remembrance that being a procrastinator will always prevent you from acquiring the power that is needed to bring about change that can one day make the world a better place. Despite what you think, there are people rooting for you to win big. It's entirely up to you whether or not you will choose to perform like a winner or continue to aimlessly mope around like a loser.

....

He who has no power,
depends on he who has it.

—AKAN PROVERB

....

There will never be a time more ripe than the present. Today life is one day shorter than it was yesterday. There will never be a perfect time to get started. Jump in and create something before it becomes too late. After the time has passed by, you will be filled with a never-ending sorrow. Don't worry about what you don't have; just focus on trying to understand that, as you progress, greater opportunities will come your way, unless you have already been ruined by being a procrastinator.

 **JEWEL**

Do not allow procrastination to become your down fall.

Anything in Life Is Possible

The pessimist says, "It can't be done."
The optimist says, "I just did it."

—AUTHOR UNKNOWN

THERE WAS ONCE a school teacher who, each morning, would wait until her class was through reciting the Pledge of Allegiance before modestly reminding them, "Students, do not squander the value of your day by forgetting to eliminate the barriers of your imagination!" What insightful wisdom Mrs. Parker had. That lady was brilliant.

Each day, after Mrs. Parker had finished instructing our class, she would spend the remainder of the course discussing "the infinite possibilities of life."

May God bless her soul. It has been almost ten years since her unfortunate passing. Often, I find myself contemplating the importance of the lessons she provided to us. In rare moments of solitude, I can envision Mrs. Parker patting me on the back in a motherly-like fashion while warmly lecturing all of us on the significance of utilizing our imaginations and becoming conscious of the power that lies inside of our ideas. Mrs. Parker once slammed her ruler on my desk and said, "Young man! Anything in life is possible if you embrace the courage that it will take to introduce your ideas to the world. Do you understand what I am saying to you, Mr. Crawford?" To which I humbly responded, "Yes, ma'am. I understand everything you have tried so hard to teach me, Mrs. Parker. Even when I act like I'm not paying attention, I am taking heed."

She would go on to say, "If you are able to conceive a thing, regardless of what it is, you can achieve it. Everything in existence was once just a figment of someone's imagination. The mere thought of an idea is nothing other than raw energy. When you trifle with an idea, it emboldens itself with power that will never lose its elasticity. Proof? Think of how long ago the pyramid of Giza was built. Before its physical existence, it was just an idea in someone's mind. Am I correct?" I acknowledged her by appreciatively responding, "Yes, ma'am." Mrs. Parker pointed to a geographical map hanging on the wall and went on to say, "As you well know, thousands of years later the pyramids continue to awe tourists from all walks of life.

"If you coax an idea long enough, it will transform and develop a sustaining power that will mobilize you to take action. Give thought to the process of planting a seed. When you plant seeds (ideas) in fertile soil (your mind), every week you toil the garden to rid it of pests and weeds (refrain from entertaining negative influences—people, polluted music, and unproductive television). Next, you'll have to water the newly planted seeds (nourish your mind with substantive things). Don't disturb the process. Have a little faith, and in due time you will witness blooming flowers (your ideas come to fruition). It will provide you with a wonderful sense of accomplishment. This is the power in believing that all things are possible!"

At this very second, you of all people should know that behind each of your thoughts lies a tremendous force. A very valuable force that is more powerful than you know. Listen to me. Endless possibilities, thinking big, and thinking outside of the box are all about unleashing the creativity of your imagination. Stop looking at things from the same viewpoint as everyone else. Try something a bit unorthodox. Spend time learning how you can get rid of the harness that restrains your creativity. When you look at an object, your vision should be more creative than those who can only see what is presented to them on the surface.

Perhaps what appears to be an ordinary looking box to you equates to the invention of a futuristic cooling system for, let's say, NASA. This, my friend, is the type of idea that turns up when you sift through the imagination of a dreamer. When you toy around with different aspects of your imagination in terms of what's possible, you will have to abandon any limitations of conformity you may have. Just because people unanimously agree that an object is what the standards say it is doesn't mean the creativity of your imagination precludes you from conjuring up something much greater.

Allow me to pose a question. When we were so preoccupied with doing wrong, scheming and plotting for all the wrong reasons, and trying to pull one over on others, how is it that we were able to come up with so many ideas? Each time we looked around, we discovered something that provided us with an idea for how we could quickly obtain the things that best suited our selfish desires. We knew what our objectives were, and we certainly had more than enough ways to accomplish our goals. In our minds we thought, "I can fast talk Sabrena out of five hundred dollars, gamble with two hundred and fifty of that, and hopefully, I can turn it into seven hundred and fifty dollars. Then I can take that and go buy ..." You know the routine! Stop pretending as if you don't know the moral to the story.

The point is, you can do whatever you put your mind to. Don't get cold feet now that the pressure is on you to create something positive. Exert your intelligence. Let's see how many constructive ideas you can conceive in such a short period of time.

....

It always seems impossible
until it's done.

—NELSON MANDELA
....

If you fail, try again. There is no time for wallowing and crying about what could have been. Get up, dust your clothes off, and intensify your efforts, but this time, let it be with a complete understanding of where you went wrong.

Upon succeeding, remember to say, "It was possible!" Of course your success didn't come without invaluable lessons, but respect can be found in the fact that you were able to make the proper adjustments while remaining focused on your overall objective. Now you can smile with thoughts of how it was all worthwhile. You can make any of your dreams come to fruition if you remember the lesson of all things being possible.

....

Keep away from people who belittle your ambitions. Small people always do that, but the really great make you feel that you, too, can become great.

— MARK TWAIN

....

Nothing in life is a walk in the park. Obstacles will always be part of the infrastructure in a complex world, but if you go into a situation equipped with knowledge and an understanding of the beauty of what may be possible, the sun will suddenly become brighter.

It's up to you to equip yourself with a competent navigational device that will lessen the chances you have of embarrassingly crashing into things that are right in front of your face. The obvious isn't always so colorful, and for that reason alone, you must strive to become a sailor with excellent vision. When you begin to use your mind to contemplate possibilities, life will no longer be so difficult.

It's not uncommon for your journey to beat you up so new possibilities may be extracted from your wounds. If you were to never go through anything challenging, suffer temporary defeats, or feel the pain of discouragement, you would never find yourself in a position to hone your revolutionizing ideas. What do you really think imagination is about? Would you like a hint? It's about developing the courage to nurse your boundless ideas. Through uncultivated imagination, ideas are born every single day. Let's see what you can come up with.

JEWEL

Don't ever allow anyone to convince you that you can't do what your heart desires!

Not Every Friendship Is Worth Pursuing

By the time you have pushed your way through the crowd, fought to defend your integrity, and proven you are who you say, what will you have left to give?

—CHRISTIAN GARCIA

YOUR VALUE IS something worth singing about. It consists of melodies that bring genuine joy to the hearts of those of us who have never experienced such impressionable tunes. No, silly, I'm not trying to charm you. It is an offering of pleasurable commonalities from the sincerity of one heart to another in hopes of reminding you that you don't have to chase anything that was never any good for you from the beginning.

God places certain people in our lives for a reason. Some will add to your life and some will selfishly try to deny you the right to be happy. The difference between someone helping to create happiness and someone who wishes to see you down should be apparent. You can sense it. When a person with good intentions truly cares about you, that person's deeds will be an accurate reflection of what's in his/her heart: They will want for you what they want for themselves. In fact, they will want more for you than they want for themselves because had the shoe been on the other foot, they know deep within their soul that you would go an extra mile to make sure that they are okay.

When a person continuously brings toxic waste to your doorstep, what could they possibly offer you that would be beneficial? A warmhearted person would never intentionally add bad energy to the darkness that you're already struggling to push your way through.

Gossiping, complaining, acting childishly, and being jealous are all characteristics of a mean-spirited person. Look in the mirror. Do you see the smile that radiantly shines with such great potential? So what if you have a few issues. We all do. It's those who are afraid to admit they have flaws who will take the longest to heal. You are blessed. Stop acting like you are waiting for someone in particular to validate your worth. No one, except for your parents, knows how to love you better than you know how to love yourself. There is a strong likelihood that someday someone special may become capable of loving you the way you deserve, but not before you have a chance to teach that person how to be gentle with the portion of your heart that needs extra attention.

May I remind you of something? Never pursue people who are incapable of being reciprocal, thoughtful, or infused with a positive outlook that can assist you in growing mentally, emotionally, and spiritually. There is nothing that anyone can offer you that should come at the expense of causing you to feel as though you were begging them for anything. With God's help, you have been self-sustaining for thousands of years. That's right, you! Hasn't anyone ever told you that your strength invokes a smile in the hearts of those who are complementary of you? It is you who promotes loyalty while sprinkling a little bit of praise on those of us who are deserving. You heal in a way that could never be duplicated by anyone other than another strong person. You have carried us on your back when we badly wanted to fall down crying for additional strength to keep pressing on. Thank you for your many, many sacrifices. Without you, what would we be?

Please, do not ever forget to call upon your Lord when you find yourself experiencing periods of vagueness. For there is no friendship more worthy of your loyalty than his. In your moments of temporary emptiness, God is preparing you for the climb to the next level. Don't believe in the actions of people who talk too much. Reliance on their words or promised deeds will do nothing more than leave you feeling resentful and frustrated. Never force yourself to be anyplace your heart has made you feel that you are unwanted. More than likely, you are in a position that others wish they occupied, but instead of them working as hard as you have, they have jealously attempted to block your blessings. But guess what? Because you have spiritual fortitude, God already has your portion of blessings reserved. Some people will never be worthy of your companionship. Don't look too deeply into the situation; it's God's way of telling us we need to spend a little more time evaluating ourselves.

Sit someplace quiet and spend time thinking about the quality of peace that certain people bring to your life. Does it recharge you? Is it healing? Does it comfort you, or at least help you to smile on the days when you do not feel like sharing your love with the world? No? Well, that settles it. It's time for you to let go and move on.

When we decide to permanently walk away from those who have honestly never been any good for us, God will be smiling, waiting to bless us with a friendship with someone who is ten times better than what we had.

Try to keep this in mind: No one can be a better friend to you than the person who proves to you how much you mean to them. Always watch with your eyes, and listen with your heart; if the two exist in unison, you may have something worth holding on to for a lifetime.

 **JEWEL**

Do not ever allow anyone to treat you as if you were a mangy dog running in circles while trying to catch its tail.

The Magical Effects of Charisma

Whether evaluating the traits of a
disciplined man, or the emotions of
a woman with great integrity, neither
is capable of being more tranquil
than the person who exudes charm.

—JOSHUA MOSES

AH, THE ALLURE of the soul. It feels almost magical. What exactly is it? It's personal magnetism. Some people have it and some people don't.

Everyone has an aura that is impregnated with accurate details of who they are. Those who have charisma are very likable. So likable that, oftentimes, we find ourselves giving and doing things for them without fully understanding the reasons why.

Have you ever been in the presence of someone you barely knew, yet felt as if you had known them for what seemed like forever? Being in their presence caused you to feel completely comfortable. It was as if you didn't have a single worry in the world. Maybe you even found yourself entertaining the thought, "I don't quite know how to describe it, but there's something about him/her that I can't explain."

People with charisma have an ability to quickly win you over. They are compassionate, sensitive, and very thoughtful. It's as if nothing means too much to them. Some are really smooth talkers, while others barely speak at all. They have a way of reminding you that you're alive. Life suddenly becomes more exciting. When a charismatic individual engages in a conversation, they tend to communicate from the core of their soul, leaving you hungry for just a little bit more of their time. Their physical features don't necessarily have to appeal to your taste for them to have charisma, but the beauty of their personality will casts a spell over you that will cause you to see nothing less than their exquisiteness.

Be sure to never allow a person with charm to persuade you to do anything you know in your heart to be wrong. Just because a person is popular doesn't mean his/her intentions do not have to be scrutinized.

Charisma will only take you part of the way; you will need to possess character and common sense to get to where you have to go in the world.

 **JEWEL**

Give very little
attention to the
glamour of words.
Silent deeds are
more appealing.

Tears of Discomfort

Warnings of caution, feelings of embarrassment and, certainly, any sense of regret for keeping your pain silent for so long, requires no explanation when the time has arrived for cleansing your soul.

—SHARDA CHEESEBORO

GO AHEAD, CRY. Let it out. For far too long you have endured pain that stems from inconsideration of your feelings, people misconstruing your intentions, and basking in shame for doing nothing other than trying hard to help those who have caused you unbelievable sadness—tears of resentment and sleepless nights filled with anguish that was supposed to have been inspirational joy somewhere along the line. Although it's extremely overwhelming, you must stay strong. Take a deep breath. It will all work out just fine.

Forgive them for their disrespect to you. Their habit of callously looking beyond your encouraging words and your supportive touch has to be extremely hurtful. The comfort of your companionship alone is praiseworthy. Your ability to share your last, even when you really don't have it to spare, is nothing less than considerate. Hey, wipe those pretty tears. It's not you. It is them. Some people are and will continue to be psychologically malnourished forever. It is God's way of showing us who's unpolished. Recently, I offered a prayer asking for those who are discourteous to be granted a chance to change. God answered by stating that he has not provided them with an appropriate cure for a reason. Such people are meant to serve as an example to humanity. An example tainted with a demonic darkness that's capable of causing your character irreparable harm. If you don't believe it, make time to reflect on the valuable moments you've spent trying to help certain people become better.

Look around! You have a lot of important things going on for yourself and you can smile with appreciation. At some point in our lives, we have all gravitated towards people who acted as if they had potential but ended up causing us to be burdened with stress and depression. It is not entirely your fault that you have spent more days crying than smiling, or trying to figure out why it is so difficult for you to express the joy of your happiness. Be thankful for your many blessings. You have been given a chance to put things back in order in a way that will help you to gradually move past your pain of yesterday. No, it won't be easy, but I assure you, once you take the first step, you will be well on your way.

Would you like to know something pretty remarkable? You have strength! There is no one who can teach you how to hold on better than you already know how. You have been doing it gracefully ever since you were taught the concept.

When real men witness you crying, we want nothing more than to run to your aid with deep concern for what's troubling you. A light rub on your back with whispered assurances that all will work out fine seems to always invoke a confident smile on your face.

From this day forward, try giving a pass to those who pretend as if your emotional displeasures are unnecessary. What could they possibly tell you about what you have been going through for such a long time? No one seems to have a problem when you work tirelessly to make certain that everyone you love has something to help them feel better about themselves. What about how you perform like a true team player without receiving so much as a "thank you" in return? Not once have you complained. Who can forget the nights you come home with a stiff back, swollen feet, and a stubbornness to only accept a small portion of dinner because you want to make sure that everyone else is adequately fed? Now it's a problem because you feel a need to cry your little heart out?

It's okay. When we weep, it is God's way of allowing us to cleanse our souls. There's no need to beat yourself up worrying about what you may have done wrong. Think about all the things you have done right. If there is something that really bothers you, consider looking at the ingratitude of those shallow souls who only wish to run around with their hands extended, as if somebody owes them something. As if you don't deserve a break from their insanity, in an attempt to regain the stability of your own life.

Let me tell you something. Make sure you say your prayers, wash your face from those countless hours of crying, and pull yourself together. Don't force something that was never meant to be. You experienced the unpleasantness of their lack of concern, their harsh words, and their refusals to do better. There is nothing left. Now you must gather the strength to go your own way; if not, your feelings, your dreams, and your ability to be independent will get stepped on in a manner that will render you incapable of helping yourself or anyone else. Remember your worth. Once you have done so, be certain that it retains a value that will never allow you to forget who you are and for what reason you find yourself shedding precious tears.

JEWEL

When you feel down and out, do something, anything, for someone else. It will help you feel so much better.

Strive To Be a Little More Realistic

....
It is nothing other than a
corrupted heart, that continuously
persuades man to relish in the
falsehoods of their imagination.

—JEANETTE CHEVAS
....

MANY OF US indignantly stroll through life preoccupied with notions of being so realistic, while effortlessly casting noose after noose of judgement around the necks of those whose sensibility has yet to fully mature. How impractical is that?

Allow me a minute of your time so that I may pull your coat on something important. Being realistic means you have a mindset that unequivocally respects the boundaries of what is not only feasible, but also authentic. There is absolutely no space for the false narrations of your wild imagination, nor patience for the exaggerated emphasis you continually place on things you're "supposedly" going to do.

Consider this hypothetical situation: Back in high school, there was a guy who everyone knew by the name of "Bull." Unbeknownst to him, we called him Bull because he was full of it. He never saw the point in taking advantage of what school had to offer; instead, he chose to be a class clown, cracking jokes, talking excessively when he should have been paying attention, and always overpainting his accomplishments. Silly kid!

One day, Bull bit off more than his personality could handle. I will never forget this story for as long as I live. It was a warm spring afternoon. Rather than eating lunch in the school cafeteria, the principal, Mrs. Miller, gave us permission to have lunch in the outside courtyard.

Bull thought he was God's gift to women. His first mistake came when he interrupted Re'Nee Taylor while she was studying for an upcoming math exam. Without so much as an "excuse me," Bull tapped Re'Nee on her shoulder and said, "Do you mind if I ask you a serious question?" Re'Nee irritatingly snapped, "It better be important!" Bull had an awfully bad habit of thinking that everyone was up for his buffoonery. He sheepishly said, "I just want to know if I can have your phone number?" In that instant, I knew what had been a pleasant lunch thus far was about to turn into a come-to-Jesus moment. Man, when I used to hear an older person speak in such a manner, I knew someone was in for a rude awakening.

Anyone who was familiar with Re'Nee knew she took her studies seriously. She was on course to graduate high school six months after her sixteenth birthday. Re'Nee had aspirations to someday follow in the footsteps of former secretary of state Condoleezza Rice.

Bull cracked a silly lookin' smile, revealing his lifeless, chipped tooth, and said something to the effect of, "Stop playing hard to get! You know you wanna give me a play." That was the last straw for Re'Nee. She slammed her book shut and lunged so close to Bull's face, their noses almost touched. If you could have seen the fear in Bull's eyes … He looked as if he was about to get a verbal beating from his grandmother.

Re'Nee was so frustrated by his antics, she began to cry. In no uncertain terms she screamed, "Give you a play? Just what does that even mean? Every day, you come to school talking about people, clowning around, and telling bold-faced lies to whoever is stupid enough to listen. For some strange reason you seem to think everything is a game. If I were to offer you an incentive, you couldn't even provide me with an answer to a math equation as simple as, what's the square root of one hundred? How dare you disrespect me by asking such a childish question? If my mother and father ever had a clue that I was interested in someone as pitiful as you, they would immediately disown me. Well, not necessarily disown me, but they would certainly be unforgiving. Here I am, studying my butt off, trying to make something of my life, and you stand here looking totally clueless!" Re'Nee wiped the tears from her eyes and went on to say, "Listen, Bull! I don't know what you take me to be, but I resent you intentionally trying to interfere with my education. There are plenty of girls prancing around here, acting shallow and brainless! I am definitely not one of them. I don't come to school seeking a chance to be the center of attention. I am a focused young woman who knows the importance of handling my business, being prompt, accepting responsibility for my actions, and being a thinker, opposed to acting like a fool. Keep acting like you don't need an education and you are going to find yourself locked inside of a steel cage. You better wake up and get with the program before it becomes too late. From now on, if you don't have anything constructive to say to me, just don't say anything at all.

"As a matter-of-fact, against my better judgement, I am going to leave you with something valuable to think about. I don't have to personally know you to see you have a few issues that you need to address. The reason why I flipped out on you is because every single one of us has been handpicked to attend this school, but you act like you don't even care. I am sure your mother would be furious if she knew how you carry on, on a daily basis. Tighten up and stop taking everything for granted. There are plenty of kids out there who wish they had a chance to receive the education that we are getting here. Let me tell you something else, I have no interest whatsoever in becoming intimately familiar with anyone before I become accomplished."

Bull extended his hand to Re'nee and said softly, "I can appreciate everything you said to me. Although it was a bit harsh, I respect it! No one has ever given me constructive criticism the way you have. I guess I was too busy pretending to be all of the things I wasn't. My feelings are slightly bruised, but I honestly think it's what I needed. Thank you, Re'Nee, for being real with me."

She said, "It's no problem. That's what anyone who's realistic would do for a fellow classmate. Oh, one more thing, stop allowing people to call you Bull. Your mother named you Hezekiah. It's a beautiful name. Perhaps that is where you may want to begin your personal transformation. Discover who you really are and embrace it. Hold onto it dearly. Polish it so it has a viable chance to shine as bright as the North Star."

A realistic person understands his/her strengths, capabilities, and limitations. Biting off more than you're able to chew can destroy valuable relationships, relationships that aren't so easy to come by anymore. Furthermore, when you take on more than you can handle, it carries the risk of causing people to second-guess your motives. Why even put yourself through such emotional turmoil when it's much easier to lay your cards on the table for everyone to see? This thing called life is serious. It comes with an abundance of responsibilities that are anything but a joke. If you decide to waste your life playing games, let it be at your own expense. You don't have a right to obstruct other people's creative processes. Try providing folks with an opportunity to genuinely evaluate what you have to offer or, simply, keep moving along. If this is the course you choose to take, at least you can't be accused of being anything less than real. It will be your truth and your reality. One that you didn't feel a need to exceed the boundaries of. Whether you agree with it or not, real is real. Don't force yourself on anyone. Building a genuine alliance has to come naturally, not at the expense of your character being tainted because you decide to ignore the wisdom of how to play your part.

Truth? We all enjoy being the superhero in some capacity, but don't lose sight of the fact that your first allegiance is to yourself. Before you can think about being real with others, you must first know how to be real with yourself. If you don't have any value in the words you speak or confidence in what you are able to do, why should anyone else? The world is full of people who do nothing more than act animated and profess to be some of this, sprinkled with a little of that, every single day! How is it possible? When you find a moment to sit back and reflect on it, you have to admit it is embarrassing. Such fine talent, but we would rather waste it on discussing nonsense. Here it is: people have continually tried so hard to give us the benefit of the doubt, but in the end, all they are left with is a feeling of resignation. Entirely too many of us waste precious time pretending to be more than we are and acting as if we are extravagantly capable of doing more than we even care to attempt. That's not realistic. The professionals see your act coming two miles in advance. Tighten up; we're looking sloppy in the eyes of family, friends, and true spectators.

The moral of this lesson is, be yourself. You don't have to pretend to be something you're not just to be noticed. Do what you are certain you can do, and afterwards, if you feel as though you're able to do more, go for it! No one who is making something happen in life wants to waste their time or resources on someone who is foolishly unreasonable.

JEWEL

Being realistic doesn't excite people's expectations; it appropriately highlights the value of a worthy character.

—DAVID LEE

Conclusion

NOW THAT WASN'T so bad, was it? No ill intentions whatsoever. All I wanted to do was dispense a few encouraging words to people for the purpose of healing. Hopefully you have gained something memorable that will place a smile on your face. Forget about the hurtful things people say; they're just upset that you're a decent person with class.

For entirely too long, you have been dishonored and overlooked. No one can claim to care about our current condition if they have stubbornly chosen to sit in a corner with absolutely nothing intellectual to contribute to the injustices against our nature. As I look around, I find myself surrounded by people who have no compassion to forgive and certainly no desire to show someone else a better way to go. But it has not prevented me from looking within myself in hopes of discovering something meaningful that may be beneficial to the next man, woman, or child.

This book is what I feel should be in honor of you all. I know you sometimes forget that everyone has something to offer, but writing is something that I have passionately wanted to do for a very long time. I'll keep writing, I promise.

Please do not take anything that I've written as disrespectful or insensitive. If you knew my story, maybe you'd be more comfortable with my perspective and contribution.

If you survived a traumatic experience, I would like for you to know that the value of your self-esteem is a guiding light for how we all should carry ourselves. Your loyalty—you are a wonderful example of what it means to be faithful. Your commitment is extremely comforting. Fidelity would be meaningless if it weren't for your willingness to show us the way. Your generosity—it is you who hastily extends a hand, absent selfish thoughts of what you might receive in return. It is golden, and to the right people, it demonstrates your passionate concern for us all. Your gratitude— a smile. It is warming to those of us who sometimes don't have much to offer outside of helping your emotional stability. It's the little things that mean so much to you, and that is the essence of your gratitude. Your compassion to forgive even those who may not be worthy—you are human too. People have a tendency to test your boundaries without any concern for inflicting damaging pain.

Although this must be extremely nerve-wracking, you are appreciated for never forfeiting your ability to be sincerely forgiving. Your endless love—such a small word packed with enormous meaning. You have taught us that when searching for it, all we have to do is look within and find the courage to express the beauty of our minds, and the meaning of true love will become abundantly clear. Your power—it is immeasurable. It feels good knowing that you will always pull your share of the weight, plus a little more if you have to. You are willing to make changes, even though I understand I am the last person to judge anyone. Some of us require more instructions than others. This book is not a reflection of where you're at in life. It's a safety net that covers all bases in case someone picks up the book who knows nothing at all. I pray that some day this contribution may be worthy of standing amongst the memorable books of our time, but until then, I am gratified knowing my message was intellectually prepared in hopes that it may be found worthy of extending to someone who may need to be reminded of his or her potential.

Listen, some people will pretend as though your accomplishments aren't monumental. As if they would prefer for you to continue feeling leery of openly discussing the woes of your plight. Don't be sad. Hold your head up. I have each and every one of your backs. Between you and me, I've been observing people from a distance for some time now; let me tell you something: there will always be people in designated places who care enough about you to put forth the effort to make sure that you have what you need in order to continue striving.

Would you like to know what's really in this for me? A chance to see you all prosper. The grandparents of the world worry about how far we'll make it. I have accepted the task of being the conductor of this train, and I would like to leave you with this: no one is more understanding than you. When listening, somehow you manage to do it with true concern for the nature of those who might feel a bit uncomfortable. This is what adds a sparkle to your uncompromising force. Your brilliance is astonishing. Only you know how to fashionably coordinate everything! Without your alliance with Mother Nature, the world would be uninteresting. And your dignity is decent.

Once you have committed to something, there is very little that will hinder you from accomplishing your goal. That's honorable. May God always feel a need to bless the ground you walk upon. Never lose sight of how important you are and have always been to civilization. This book is proof that someone else can be counted on to deliver your message.

Traits and Emotions of a Salvageable Soul,
Volume II, coming soon.

CPSIA information can be obtained
at www.ICGtesting.com
Printed in the USA
BVHW042020110819
555625BV00006B/179/P